# Tales for Advent and Christmas

A Collection of Traditions, Stories and Customs for the Christmas Season

By

## J. Traveler Pelton

POTPOURRI
PUBLISHING

# COPYRIGHT

Tales for Advent and Christmas

A Collection of traditions, stories and customs for the Christmas Season

Copyright© November 2019

Independently published by Potpourri Publishing

Cover design by BecaCovers
Edited by Write Useful

Printed in the United States of America
First Edition published November 2019
Books> non-fiction-Christian mythology
ISBN- 9781710374216

Dedication

First, to my God and Creator, Savior and Guide, who gives us dreams and tasks, hammering our souls into shape as I hammer metal into useful instruments. May we place ourselves in His forge and let Him work. May this little work lead us closer during this season of hope.

I dedicate with love to all those who have been to the shadowy edge of life, looked over and decided to come back and try again. I've been there, I came back.

I dedicate it to my ancestors who walked the Red Road before me. Someday we will all walk the Skylands together. Until then our heart beats with the drum of unity and peace.

May God grant us the courage to live with whatever life sends us, and overcome it always with His peace.

May you keep the warmth of Christmas and the love of family in your hearts always.

# Other Books by Traveler Pelton

## Spiritual Works

- God Wanted to Write a Bestseller
- Big God, Little Me
- Lenten Stories for God's Little Children
- Natural Morning
- Ninety Days to The God Habit
- Tales for Advent and Christmas

## Christian Literary Science Fiction

The First Oberllyn Family Trilogy: The Past

- The Oberllyn's Overland: 1855-1862
- Terrorists, Traitors and Spies 1900- 1990
- Rebooting the Oberllyn's 2015-2020

The Second Oberllyn Family Trilogy: The Present

- The Infant Conspiracy
- Kai Dante's Stratagem
- The Obligation of Being Oberllyn

The Third Oberllyn Family Trilogy: The Future

- To Protect One's Own
- The Importance of Family Ties
- Kith and Kin, Together Again

## Family History
- Journey to Springhaven

**In Collaboration with T. Bear Pelton:**
- Clan Falconer's War
- The Rise of the Rebellion
- Changeling's Clan
- Forged in Water and Fire

## Other Authors Associated with Potpourri Publishing

## Lynette Spencer of Write Useful

- Basic Sewing on a Budget
- Vegetarian Cooking on a Budget

**Dan Pelton**

The Majestic Spectrum of God's Love

# Christmas -Why do we Do the Things We do?

Christmas means so many things to so many people; from those of us who have memories of our own homes and how we once celebrated, of good times with friends all the way to the other end of the spectrum with sad feelings when things didn't come up to our dreams and imaginings, or worse yet, were harsh times. In this small volume, I am trying to gather together some of the traditions, legends and stories around Christmas; and help us all to understand how we got here, from candy canes to pickles, snow to fir trees, when all that actually happened was a special baby born to a poor family two thousand years ago who simply changed the world.

The stories are divided into one reading a day starting with December 1. Twenty-five traditions, twenty-five stories that can be used as devotionals, bedtime stories, or just fun to read. It is my prayer that they help you to get closer to that Baby born centuries ago, so misunderstood, and so needed today.

After the stories are done, I share some of the food and carols that have been special to our family over the years. I also invite you to review our books and gift you with some chapters from our books. I hope you have a wonderful Christmas season, a grand New Year, and my advice to you this season as a counselor and a grandma is to remember to serve others for in doing so, you make yourself happy and spread the peace that is so much a part of good living.

# Table of Contents

# Day One
## The Tradition of a White Christmas, an Allegory

Centuries ago there was a king who was loved by his people for his wisdom, honesty and justice. Everyone in the kingdom knew they could depend on him in hard times and in good times to give mercy and show kindness to them. He was never so busy with governing that he could not stop to greet the children when he rode past. He often walked out in secret to someone's house who had had a bad time of it, gifting them quietly and telling them not to gossip about it, just accept his help. His people loved him. No one was in severe want in his kingdom; though perhaps not rich, they had all they needed.

The King, who was born the day before Christmas, and was a deeply religious man who spent a quiet hour at the beginning of each day on his knees, asking the Good Lord how best to lead his people. In return, the people, seeing this example, felt great affection for their monarch and followed his example of piety. As a result, there was very little crime in the Kingdom, it was safe for everyone and they all felt it was due to their great, good King.

One day the people began to discuss ways they could show the King honor and express their appreciation for all that he had done for them. They decided to make his next birthday the grandest one ever held anywhere.

Of course, they had celebrated for the King before, but this year would be different. They wanted their gifts to show the King just how much they loved him for his piety and kindness. They wanted their gifts to be the best and purest of any gifts they had ever given. It was decided that each gift, in keeping with the idea of purity, would be white. They all went about making gifts for the King.

Now the King heard about the plan going on and was touched by their love and loyalty. He decided that he would do his part to carry out the idea and let his people know how much he appreciated their thoughtfulness. He called his servants and they began to work as well.

There was excitement in the land as the King's birthday drew near. Every gift was to be the best that person could offer, from the lowest goose boy to the merchants and the dukes and duchesses. The day of his birthday dawned on the day of Christmas Eve and it seemed even nature cooperated as a light snow had fallen, drifting and covering the kingdom with a comforter of white. The people came in from all over the land, carrying their white gifts. To their astonishment, they were ushered into the largest room in the palace. As they came in to gift the King, at first they were stunned into silence, because the room had been done over into a purely white room- the floor was white marble; the ceiling was covered in white wool that looked like a mass of soft, white fluffy clouds; the walls were hung with beautiful white silk draperies, and all the furnishings were white. At one end of the room stood a white throne, and seated upon it was their King and he was dressed in shining white satin robes, trimmed in white ermine and his attendants dressed in white linen surrounded him. The only color was his golden crown and his scepter of office, shining with emeralds and rubies and sapphires, sparkling in the firelight against the whiteness. It was awe inspiring.

And the gifts were brought and they varied widely, just as today. In those days, just as now, there were many people who had great wealth, and they brought gifts which were generous in proportion to their wealth or lack of it.

One merchant brought a box of pearls, another a number of carved ivories. There were beautiful laces and silks and

16

embroideries, all in pure white, and splendid white porcelain chargers were brought to his majesty, carrying white divinity candy, marshmallows and white mints. The King acknowledged the gifts and had them set upon a long presentation table to the side. He gave to each one who came a token gold coin on a leather thong, showing they were his people, members of his kingdom and protected and cared for by him. Rich or poor, they received the same gift. All felt it an honor to wear.

But many of the people were poor and their gifts were quite different than the merchants and princes. Some of the families brought only handfuls of white rice in small baskets, others brought white yarn they had handspun, some of the boys brought their favorite white fantail pigeons, and one little girl smilingly gave him a pure white rose she carefully tended in her mother's garden. The King had a clear vase brought especially for it, and he placed it in the vase and kept it beside him on a small table that sat next to the throne. When she came forward for her token, the King gave her a hug and a kiss on her cheek and spoke a moment to her. She smiled and happily ran back to her mother.

It was wonderful to watch the King as each person came and knelt before Him, offering his gift of love. The King never seemed to notice whether the gift was great or small. He accepted them all, he thanked the bearer of the gift. He presented them with their token. Their beloved King was so happy that his people would honor him this way that the people decided to have a White Day every year. So it came to pass that year after year on the King's birthday the people came from everywhere and brought their white gifts which showed that their love was pure, strong, and true and year after year the King sat in his white robes on the white throne in the great white room and he accepted each person and their gift graciously and acknowledged they belonged to him.

So from that day until this, we have always wished for a White Birthday for our King, we are happy to see the snow that falls and blesses us with a White Christmas, just for Him, and we gift each other as He has gifted us each year. He accepts us no matter how poor we are, and he blesses us with His mercy and grace all the year.

"Snow flurries began to fall and they swirled around people's legs like house cats. It was magical, this snow globe world."
— **Sarah Addison Allen**

# Day Two
# The Little Old Grandmother of Russia

Many countries have customs surrounding Christmas and we're going to explore the why behind some of them. One of the most common customs is the giving of gifts. In Russia, they say it all started with a little old lady named Babushka.

Babushka, meaning 'grandmother' or 'old woman' in Russian, lived all alone in a big house, safe and warm. Her needs were simple, she grew her food, she cooked her food, she had a warm, comfortable bed, and firewood set up for the winter. During the long cold nights, she was especially lonely, for she lived far outside the town, and she had no relatives to visit, no neighbors, no friends. During the summer and fall, she would occasionally hear the sound of people traveling past in carts, and she would provide food to their animals and offer a resting place to weary travelers. She fed the wild birds that came to her feeders, and she left out hay for the local deer. Other than that, there was no one. The loneliness was an agony sometimes, a burning inside her.

When winter would come and no one came by during the long cold, dark winter, she had to stay inside all the time. The wild birds had flown south, the deer hid from wolves and there were no travelers as the wind howled outside and the snows got deep and cold. Babushka prayed for company. On one such winter night, when she was trying to sleep, she heard a noise steadily growing closer - voices and grunts and grumbles and she knew there were no people or animals for miles around on a night like this. The roads were covered in drifts of snow. There came a loud pounding at her door and she rushed to open it, thinking that it must be a desperately cold and weary group, to have to be traveling in this weather. To her astonished eyes, three white horses with three noblemen dressed in the finest and richest clothes that she had ever seen stood in front of her house. She tried to usher them in out of the cold at once.

"Oh, you are so cold, so weary! Please come in, come in. Your servant can take the animals to my stable, there is hay there and grain, and the water well not far to draw from to give them to drink. Come, now, my fire is warm."

"We may not," said the first Wise man, for that is who they were. "We travel far to come to the side of the infant King."

"What King is this?" she asked him. "Surely you can wait the night and go when the storm is over? It is so dark and so cold."

"No," said the Second Wise Man. "The King we seek is of this world and not of this world. He needs our gifts to help him accomplish his task. We must make haste. But good woman, he would have a loving grandmother near to help his mother, to cuddle him as a grandchild and keep him safe and warm. Will you come with us? There is room, here, on my servant's donkey for you to ride, so it will not be a long journey. The Infant invites you to come to Bethlehem. He calls us, and we cannot delay to rest for we must go far this night."

"What nonsense is this?" Babushka complained. "You cannot mean to get to Bethlehem in the Holy Land tonight. No, I cannot come! It is dark and cold and I am an old woman. Please come inside and get warm. I will heat up soup and give you bread." Despite her entreaties, the Wise men shook their head and rode off into the swirling snow and disappeared.

She closed her door on her empty house, sighed, banked her fires and went to bed. As she lay in her bed that night, listening to the wind against her shutters, she thought of the three men and the strange story they told about the child who would be a king. "I should have listened. I am a foolish old woman. I will rise in the morning, take gifts and find this child they speak of. Surely other travelers will know the way I am to go."

The next morning was clear and bright. She could barely hear the church bells far below her in the valley, ringing out the new day. Hustling around, she gathered some trinkets to gift the Baby and set out in the cold dawn of Christmas Eve day. But she could find neither the Wise men or tracks from their horses, as the storm had blown them away, and the village folk thought her mad. She gave a few gifts to the children in the village, sweet candies, cookies, what grandmother could resist? She then hustled in the direction the Wise men had gone, south. She stopped at each village to ask for directions and found that no matter how much candy and trinkets she gave to children her pack was full. It is said that the old mother is looking for the boy king to this day and that whenever she meets a child, she gifts him or her with trinkets, tells them to be good and continues on her search.

And so, in Russia, old Babushka started the custom of giving gifts to children on Christmas as the real Babushka tries to find the baby King and bring Him the comfort of a grandmother.

**Isaiah 9:6** For to us a child is born, to us a son is given; and the government shall be upon his shoulder, and his name shall be called Wonderful Counselor, Mighty God, Everlasting Father, Prince of Peace.

# Day 3
# The Three Kings or Magi of Christmas

The Three Kings or Magi or Wise Men, depending on which theologian or historian you read, traveled for hundreds of miles to see baby Jesus and bring him gifts of gold, frankincense and myrrh. Magi were scholars, priests or astrologers, and we don't really know there were three but assume that because there were three gifts mentioned, so we think they must have been three in number. Since it is likely they had an entourage (No one traveled alone in those days, much less people who would be seen as wealthy enough to own camels) the entourage could have been quite large with servants and soldiers. The Bible calls them the wise men of the east, and that they followed a star that moved.

Coming as they did from a far country, asking about a new born King, they must have caused a quite a commotion in Jerusalem.   They didn't mention he was the Messiah; they called him a King, which made Herod the Great, the actual king of that time, pretty upset.

Herod was an evil man, a deeply astute politician and ruthless to the core. When he heard about the visitors in the town, and what they were asking, he called together his counselors for data. He demanded the priests tell him everything in prophecy concerning this King. He had no intentions of giving up his throne quietly. Once he knew about Bethlehem, he called in the guests and showed off his wisdom of the ancient texts, and asked them to please bring him back word once they'd found the child so he could worship him as well. Let's join them now as they leave the court of King Herod, and travel the five or six miles down to Jerusalem that night.

"It's time we leave, your majesty," remarked the first King to Herod. The Magi Stood up as one. "Look out the window: the stars are up, and there is the Star, over Bethlehem. It's time we followed it and found the Lord."

"Excellent," beamed Herod. "I won't hold you back. Please remember to bring me word when you have found him. I'll get my gifts ready for him and wait your word; I cannot, alas, leave my governing duties, but will go when you have found the child."

The Magi went out, mounted their camels and headed towards the star, towards the little town. They had first seen the star months before, in their homeland, and now it seemed as if the long journey would come to an end. They watched the Star and it seemed to settle down over a certain small house.

They sent their servants to the house of the head elder of the small town and he told them that indeed, there had been a child born a little while before, a boy, during the last census. His parents had found no place to stay the night and ended up finding shelter in the cave stables, down below town. After the crowd for the census left, they stayed in town for the forty days needed until the child could be dedicated. They had called him Jesus, Emmanuel, which was odd since it wasn't a family name. They rented a small house off Jed, down the road there. Wasn't it bright out tonight?

The Servant ran back to his master, and told him all that had been told him.
"Born in a manger, in a stable, no place for himself on this earth. That matches the prophecy." declared one of the magi.
"And he has been dedicated in the temple at forty days old. We are here just in time, I think," said another Magi, nodding. The

others agreed and dismounted, then quietly knocked on the door the elder had spoken of to the servant.

Joseph answered the knock. He looked up in surprise at the richly dressed men.

"Is this the house where the newborn King of the Jews dwells?" asked one. "We have come from far off to the East to come and worship Him."

Mary smiled as she held her little one. He was nearly one now. The lateness of the year and the weather had forced them to stay here in Bethlehem longer than expected, and they hoped to soon be on their way home. Jesus stood as any toddler would, smiling, hanging onto Mother, sucking on a finger.
The Magi Kings came forward with their gifts and knelt, opening each one in turn.

"Gold for my Lord's journey," said the first.

"Frankincense to help him grow up strong," remarked the second.

"Myrrh to anoint him when the time comes for his sacrifice and yours; to lighten the load and the pain." said the third, older man. "Keep it safe for him."

They offered prayers and the baby gurgled and smiled and patted their shiny jewels. They rested in the house that night, and got up to leave in the morning, for they knew their group was too large for this poor family to feed and house.

As they mounted their camels, one looked at the other and said, "I do not think it is good for us to go back to the place. I do not trust that man. I had a dream last night."
The others had also felt the anger beneath the calm surface of Herod and they all had had the same dream and agreed. The

Wise men, being discerning as well as knowledgeable, rode out of Bethlehem and around Jerusalem quietly and were many miles out and away before morning.

"The Star has gone," said one. "It is time to go home and document our journey for the future." They nodded and headed out back to the East, each keeping within his heart the things they had seen of the child.

And from where we live, so many centuries later, we may wonder, aren't those odd gifts for a baby? Perhaps. But that very night an angel came to Joseph and told him to grab the child and go to Egypt, for Herod was out to kill the baby. Joseph rose in haste and was able to buy what was needed for the trip with a gold piece; food, water bags, a small cart for the donkey to pull. They left at once, just ahead of Herod's soldiers. They stayed in Egypt until Herod died, and the gold would have helped provide for the child in a foreign land. An odd thought occurs to me; since Jesus was just the step child of Joseph, but was the Son of God, was God the Father providing a form of Child Support for His Son to aid the man who would raise him?

Frankincense was not only used for incense but medicine in those days, and it could have been used to aid Mary when Jesus went through the normal illnesses that took so many lives in times before. And when Christ died, they wrapped his body in spices and linen; and it could have been the myrrh brought by the wise men so long ago. So the Wise men, the Kings, the Magi, we remember as the ones whose wise gifts supported our Lord as a baby; protected and warned him, and announced him to the royalty of the court of those days.

**Matthew 2:11** And when they had come into the house, they saw the young Child with Mary His mother, and fell down and worshiped Him. And when they had opened their treasures, they presented gifts to Him: gold, frankincense, and myrrh.

# Day Four
## Just What do Storks have to do with Christmas?

There is an old story, told for years that the stork showed
compassion on the Baby Jesus is a special way on the night of
His birth.

We all know Jesus was born in a stable, surrounded by animals,
and laid in a manger. In one tradition, there were more than just
farm animals about; for perched high up in a fir tree above the
cave stable (for most the stables around Bethlehem were made
in the caves outside the town), the stork watched the excitement
and noted the little one carefully wrapped; how Joseph filled
stone manger with hay and then settled the baby on  the hay.
The little one wiggled uncomfortably because hay is scratchy to
young baby skin. He didn't complain, but the Babe sighed a
baby sigh.

"This will simply not do," grumbled the stork. "Doesn't that
human know how to properly make a nest? Has he no mate to
show him? The child won't be comfortable on just hay.  He
won't even be warm."

The stork, being an amiable if grumpy bird and prone to act
before thinking about it, flew down and stalked into the cave

with his mate. They marched over to the baby and  Baby Jesus smiled at them sleepily. Already the hay was making itchy places on his tiny arms.

The long-legged stork looked at his mate and at the other birds in the rafters, doves and pigeons, a small wren or two.

"Come, friends!" he croaked. "Come help us make the baby warm and safe!"

The stork looked at Jesus and said softly, "I have no gift to give other than what I have and am. But what I have I give you freely, My little Lord."

The storks immediately started to pull out their breast feathers and tucked them all around the child, as they would for their own chicks. The other birds followed their lead, putting soft feathers all around and under the baby. Baby Jesus yawned, cuddled down into the soft down featherbed and fell asleep. Nodding their heads to the Mother Mary, they stalked out of the stable and back to their tree. She smiled her thanks and patted the soft bed. In her heart she asked the Great Father of Jesus to reward the storks for their kindness in providing a place for her baby to sleep. And so it is, that from that time until this, storks have been considered a symbol of prosperity and compassion, and are often seen represented at baby showers. If you see a stork flying overhead, or circling around a house, it is a lucky sign for that family (in old days, it meant an easy birth for the mother). They provided the best feather bed they could for their Infant King, and they are remembered and honored and always thought of as a patron of babies.

One of the old English tales says that the souls of unborn babies live in watery areas and as storks visit these areas frequently, they deliver the babies' souls to their parents by carrying them in a special basket and as they fly over, the soul drops down and enters the mother. In the Gaelic countries, storks are referred to as soul bearers. Only the robin is held in higher regard-but we'll get to the robin later. For now, snuggle down into your own comfy bed and think of the gift of comfort brought by one of God's creatures to His son. As legends go, it's one of the nicer ones...

Psalm 104:17 Where the birds make their nests;
The stork has her home in the fir trees.

# Day 5
# Why are Candy Canes Eaten at Christmas?

Mint hard candy has been around for centuries, mint being the easiest of herbs to grow, and flavoring things so well. However, the legend of the candy cane goes far beyond that. Let's look in on a choir practice back in the late middle ages, where the choirmaster was having a time of it.

"Hans! Simon, Pieter! Shush right now and get in your places! We need to get this music ready for the Christmas services." The boys would settle for a few minutes but as soon as the choirmaster's attention was distracted, they started acting up as boys will do when standing around in choir robes, in a cold church, bored with practicing. Christmas was almost here and there were so many other things they'd rather be doing. The choir master tried scolding, he hit their hands with a stick (that was acceptable in those days.) he pleaded. It was all useless for getting attention.

His wife, just then, came into the church with a basket. Smiling at her exasperated husband, she showed the children what she had.

"Children, for everyone who acts nicely and practices well, I will give you one of these shepherd canes" she said quietly. She held in her hand a pure white piece of hard candy, with the head bent over like a letter "J." "They may help you remember whom we sing for."
Since the children did not get candy very often, and as she stood just by the back door to watch, they trilled like little angels.

They progressed more that day than they had in weeks. The choirmaster was encouraged greatly. After the boys hung their robes, they rushed to the door where the Choirmaster's wife gave them each a candy, and promised to make more for the next practice and something extra special for performance.

Now back in those days, handing out chocolate or candy in church was considered sacrilegious. By giving the candy stick a bend, and connecting the candy stick with a Biblical symbol the grumpy old biddies in the church were appeased. It also helped that the choirmaster's wife made enough that they got one too. After all, the Shepherd's staff represents Jesus, our Great Shepherd. What could be more churchlike?

The bent candy became very popular in 1847, when a German/Swedish immigrant came to America, to Wooster, Ohio, and used them on his Christmas tree as decorations and treats. It became quite fashionable at the time. By 1900, they had acquired red stripes.

Today, it is said that the whiteness of the candy cane represents the purity of the Christ, the red represents the blood shed to save us, and the peppermint flavor is much like hyssop, which symbolizes sacrifice. It has become one of the most popular symbols of the season.

Luke 2:8
And in the same region there were shepherds out in the field, keeping watch over their flock by night.

# Day Six
## How the Sage Plant became so Useful

Remember the detour of the Wise men a few days ago? King Herod was outraged the Wise men did not come back to him. He'd waited several days, and his spies told him the Magi were gone. He was in a temper to say the least and that was not safe for anyone: this was a man who murdered his own sons, banished his first wife and son so he could marry another woman and eventually had her killed as well.

Anger infused his mind and all he could think about was getting rid of this new King. He had no way of knowing where the baby was hidden since his spies had been unable to locate the child. He made a decision, a horrible, dreadful decision. Since he couldn't find that one child, and since they knew that child had been born in Bethlehem, then if he killed all the male children in Bethlehem, he'd kill that king; after all, what were a few babies compared to the security of his throne? He knew from his talk with the Wise men that the baby would not be an infant by this time, more like a one year old, so he doubled it and decided the breaking point would be two. All male infants under the age of two he ordered murdered in one night.

Bethlehem was a small town, a few hundred residents at most, and the children would be so precious to them. It is thought that as many as twenty children were killed that night. Just in case someone tried to escape, the soldiers covered all the roads leaving or going into Bethlehem. which was pretty much in and out of the small town. They circled the town, beat the bushes and went inside, where using the new census reports made at Jesus birth (the reason they were in Bethlehem was that census) they went to specific addresses and killed babies. The Bible had foretold the entire massacre in the book of Jeremiah years before-in fact over six hundred years before…

Joseph, Mary and the baby were on the road fleeing, since they had been warned by an angel this would happen. People along the way were frightened of Romans and would not give them shelter for fear of their own safety. The road from Judea to Egypt's border was many miles, and no one trusted strangers. The mercenaries were everywhere. The holy family rushed on until they could not go farther. They had to stop to eat, nurse the baby, to drink some water, rest the poor donkey.. The old story says that Mary and Joseph heard the soldiers marching and feared they would be captured. Mary begged the Father to help them hide in the brush safely by the road while they rested. There was not a tree or a cave near and they knew the soldiers were close. They needed rest for a few hours.

There were many bushes by the roadside. There was a group of roses blooming by the road, but the rose thought they might crush her bush or flowers by squeezing under and behind them and refused them sanctuary; so now the rose has thorns that showed its' prickly attitude. Mary and Joesep turned away, saddened and tired but saw a large clove bush and hurried to try and lie down under its' branches. But the clove was too busy blooming to listen to the plea to let them rest. Therefore, the legend says, today the clove blossom is bad smelling and not useful for much. The humble sage bush offered them it's help. It felt pity on the Mother and child and moved its' branches gently

34

in the wind, offering a sweet odor and welcome. They rested under it and it quickly blossomed and stretched its' protecting branches over them. The soldiers raced by and the little family was not seen. So today, sage is used almost around the world and is considered a sacred plant; it is used in medicine and as an essential oil and it is used in cooking imparting a sweet, earthy, pine like flavor. The purple flowers grow thickly in the late spring and are edible as well. Sage is symbol of wisdom, hospitality and good health.

**Jeremiah 31:15** Thus said Jehovah, A voice in Ramah is heard, wailing, weeping most bitter, Rachel is weeping for her sons, she hath refused to be comforted for her sons, because they are not.

# Day Seven
## Spiders? Really? Why are they on my tree?

According to Ukraine folklore, on Christmas eve, the Christ child would come down to earth and bless the children of men. After everyone had gone to bed for the night, the child would enter the village, walk up and down, and where ever he was welcome, leave His blessing on that household for the next year. In preparation for this event, it was the custom centuries ago to super clean the house before the eve of Christmas so that when the Christ child should arrive to bless the family, all would be clean and ready.

Unfortunately, this meant that all the spider webs and all the dust and dirt were swept away in the cleaning frenzy. A fir tree was brought in and decorated, and thus the family was prepared to receive a visit from the Christ and hopefully a blessing.

The spiders simply could not understand why they should be relegated to the dust and chased outside to find new homes, away from the warmth of the house. One group of spiders hid out in the attic of a certain manor house. On Christmas eve, shivering in the attic, the younger spiders grumbled to the elder ones it was not fair, and they were going to go downstairs and just see what all the excitement was about. The elders listened to them, and really curious themselves, decided they would all sneak down after everyone was in bed, just before the midnight chime rang, and see what on earth was the people's problem with them. After all; did they not work hard catching insects to protect the family? Did they not thus guard them from disease by ridding the home of harmful, illness infected insects? Why were they driven out so thoroughly once a year?

Late at night, when the fires were banked and the family asleep, they dropped by web down, down, down to the largest room of the house. There they saw the Tree sitting in a corner, adorned with shiny balls and chains of berries and nuts, smelling like the forest. The spiders ran over to it, so pretty, so pretty, and they climbed into its' branches. They were so captivated by the beauty they spent all night in the tree, crawling up and down and examining its beautiful ornaments. They could not curb their urge to weave pretty and delicate spider webs all over the tree as they danced on its branches. In the wee hours of the morning, the little Christ child came to bless the house. He was so surprised to find little spiders and their webs on the tree.

The Christ child knew that every creature was made by God because He was there before when they were made. He also knew how the mother and her servants had worked hard all the week long to make everything perfect for His visit. They would be horrified to find the spider webs on their tree. He considered and then, with a smile on his lips, he reached out and touched the webs and turned them from sticky spider webs to shiny silver and gold threads. He gave his blessing to the house and in the Ukraine, they say that this is how tinsel was first made to decorate Christmas trees. Today, some folks put a spider web ornament on their tree to remember the hard work of the spiders in that long-ago year.

**Proverbs 20:38** The spider taketh hold with her hands, and is in kings' palaces.

# Day Eight
# Why Are Robins Special to Christmas?

Robins are such a cheerful little bird, yet in most of the United States, they fly south in the winter and we don't see them at Christmas, but they have a very special place in the Christmas customs of the world and especially in Great Britain.

In British folklore, the robin is said to have been in the stable when Jesus was born. He sang to entertain Mary as she labored, and once the child was delivered, and the other animals had gone to sleep after the excitement of the shepherd's visits and the angels and the star, the robin sat in the rafters, trilling softly until the baby Jesus and his Mother fell asleep. The fire that was the only source of heat in the stable burned brightly and kept them warm, but finally Joseph fell asleep as well. The robin dozed but woke with a start when something didn't seem quite right. He noticed that as the night wore on, the fire started burning down. It was dark and cold and a wind had crept into the stable cave. He hopped down to check the baby and found Him shivering in the cold but not wanting to wake His mother, had not cried out.

In an effort to keep the fire going, the little robin came close to the coals and beat his wings to fan it into flame, all the time singing shrilly. He hastily picked up straws and small twigs and dropped them on the fire to build it up. He frantically beat his wings over the embers until they flamed up. Not noticing he was too close to the fire, he kept jumping over to pick up twigs, adding them, beating his wings and singing. His efforts woke Joseph, who tended the fire.

The robin had not realized that he had gotten too close to the fire and had singed his breast feathers.

Joseph took the little bird up in his arms and thanked it for its' watch care and from the cradle, baby Jesus looked up and smiled then cuddled down into the warm of the feathers from the stork and the hay from the barn animals. The robin's breast feathers began to restore; the singed feathers dropped as if molted away; his skin underneath the feathers healed at once but now the feathers that grew out were a deep red color, like the flames it had tried to keep alive. To this day, the little robin has a red breast to show him honor for his selfless act towards the Christ child and his Mother. When the English settlers came to America, they were overjoyed to find we had robins here, just as back home, and they continued the tale, telling it to their children each year.

Today, the robin is the national bird of Great Britain. It is called the Christmas robin, robin redbreast or just robin and its' picture appear on cards, greets and calendars for Christmas.

"My idea of Christmas, whether old-fashioned or modern, is very simple: loving others. Come to think of it, why do we have to wait for Christmas to do that?" – *Bob Hope*

# Day Nine
# The Rose and the Shepherdess

We all know about the Wise men and their wonderful, expensive gifts, made just in time to give the Holy family the means to escape Herod. But folktales say there were other gifts given that night to the Christ child. After all, even today we gift the blessings that are babies with gifts when we visit them. It was the same then as now, the occasion of a birth was a joyous, happy time, even for the poor.

The Christmas Rose plant still exists and blooms from November to February and is a member of the Hellebore family, an evergreen. How it comes to bloom the opposite of all other flowering shrubs is where this legend originated. Here is what the tale says was the beginning of this intriguing little plant.

On the cold night that Jesus was born in the stable, all the shepherds came to admire and worship the new King. They were not wealthy, or able to give gifts of gold or silver; but they brought food, and a sheep skin, a simple warm supper for the parents, a small rattle for the child, the simple gifts of the poor on a happy occasion. The angels had spoken to them, that this child was for them as well as the rich; that He would save them all from their sins. They came and worshipped and showed their love as best they were able.

Now there was a shepherdess named Madelene, who was very poor. She had been able to bring nothing to the newly born king and she felt terrible about it. She only helped the other shepherds with their flocks, she was just learning to be a shepherd and she had no flock assigned to her and she had no one to appeal to for help in order to gift the baby. Had she had time, she might have been able to fashion a small basket while she worked in the fields, she might have been able to prepare a little loaf of bread, but called straight from the fields by the angels, there was nothing she could do. She felt helpless and began to softly weep in the background of the other shepherds, in the darkness at the front of the cave where she thought no one would see her. She so wanted to go in but felt unworthy without a gift. She looked up and saw the Holy Star in the heavens. She had heard the angels singing, and she felt she could do nothing. She had looked all along the way to the stable for something she could bring, even a few flowers but alas! It was cold that time of year, all the flowers were asleep for the coming winter and nothing was blooming. There was nothing she could bring.

As she stood there, afraid to go in and show her utter unworthiness, an angel guard standing by the door of the cave saw her. He took pity on the child and he looked up to the Creator with a wish for aid for this, his smallest, poorest follower. A light shown down from the heavens from the star and where her tears had fallen, just there at her feet, a plant sprang up, small, and tough and green in the cold but with clusters of soft white flowers tipped in pink. The angel softly whispered in the shepherdess's ear these were for the Christchild and his mother. She gathered them up, for they were more valuable than the gifts the Wise men would bring later, being gifted by the Father Himself for her to give to His Son. She was God's envoy to the King. They were a small miracle, made of love, the best of all gifts for the baby. She joyfully went into the cave with her bouquet and gave them to Mary for the child. Jesus, seeing the gift sent from His Father because of a young girl's love, smiled at her, because they represented all those who would love him, who were coming in later times, they were a symbol to Him that His gift to us would someday bloom like these flowers. The Christmas rose plant still grows in winter, and it symbolizes hope, love and all that is joyful and happy about Christmas.

"I wish we could put up some of the Christmas spirit in jars and open a jar of it every month." – *Harlan Miller*

*Christmas rose scientific name is hellbore niger: it is not related to true roses.

# Day Ten
# The Thorny Staff

From Great Britain comes a tale that happens on Christmas eve each year, but which did not originally start on Christmas, but 33 years later.

Two thousand years ago, after Jesus had been sacrificed for our sins on the cross, the Roman government tried to destroy his followers. One of those he tried to capture was Joseph of Arimathea who had allowed Jesus' body to lie in his burial cave for three days until His resurrection. Pilate thought Joseph had spread the story of Jesus' resurrection and if Pilate killed him as an example to all the other poor souls who believed this nonsense about a resurrection, the rumors supporting the new religion would die out, and he, Pilate, would have a lot less problems governing this really stubborn people.

Joseph of Arimathea fled from Jerusalem, carrying only his staff made of thorn wood and the Holy Grail, the one Jesus had drunk from at the Last Supper. The Grail was wrapped in pure white samite linen and was, as far as they knew, the last thing that their best Friend had used before his death. It held great significance to the early church as a reminder of his blood shed for them. Joseph wandered for miles, chased by soldiers and led by the Spirit to a safe place in Gaul (the Roman name for most of Europe.). There he was welcomed by Philip, who had traveled there to spread the Good News earlier. Philip gave him refuge for a while as he rested, but one night, refreshed from his time with Philip, Joseph had a dream sent from the Lord telling him his rest was over. In that vision, he was told to go to Britain

45

and spread the gospel. He was specifically told to speak to King Arvigarus as he had a special gift for him. Joseph was also told there would be a miracle and that the work would spread out from this new place to cover all of Britain, (which back then included Scotland and Wales. Ireland came later in the chain of events as told in tradition.)

Joseph told Philip and Philip provided him with eleven traveling companions, food, water bags and a little money for ship fare. They boarded a ship and went to Albion (Great Britain.). This faithful, humble servant of Jesus asked where the king lived and simply marched up to his throne room, explained his mission and waited. The King asked him questions, a good many questions, as it turned out, but finally deciding this was genuine, since the King had also had a vision about what was going to happen in his Kingdom. Joseph appeared to be the man in that vision sent to the King.

The King had prepared his answer to the dream, and Joseph and his followers were gifted with the Island of the Blessed, called Avalon, also known as the Happy Isle, Isle of the Glassy waters and he was told to build his altar there and his church. (This is the same Albion that was known in legend as the home of the old religion, so to go there and build a Christian alter amongst all the druid worshipers would have been a frightening endeavor.) Joseph and his followers, and some others who had decided to follow the Christ got into boats and headed for the island.

As they approached, they saw the island was surrounded by blooming water lilies and apple trees bearing bright fruit grew everywhere: it was reaping time and the local people were harvesting fruit. Avalon seemed so peaceful, was very beautiful and had good springs. They reached the Isle of Avalon on Christmas eve, tired but excited; the local people welcomed these strangers. Joseph kept gazing around, seeming to be looking for something. He stopped once and smiled, then headed up a steep hill. In the stories, the hill was called Weary-all by the local folks because the only trail up went back and forth in switchbacks, it was really steep and the gravel loose; a person would need surefootedness and stamina to even get to the first ridge without breaking his neck, but Joseph kept climbing, looking upward. He marched all the way to the top and praying out loud to God, he planted his staff in the ground with a thump, declaring this hill for the Lord and the church. Here was where they would start their grand work of spreading the Gospel.

To everyone's surprise, the staff immediately took root, grew branches, leaves and bloomed wonderful white fragrant flowers! It was the promised miracle. The followers scrambled to build an altar of surrounding rocks and a large flat stone. Here  the church was started and it was much later rebuilt and called Glastonbury Abbey. They placed the holy Grail in the chapel. It is said in Britain to this day, the thorn bush blooms at Christmas time and then in the spring, when the first convert had been baptized, it blooms again. The first church burned sometime in the fifth century; it was replaced by a larger church in the 7th century, and again in the 13th century. Parts of that third church still exists today but only as ruins. You can visit them and you can still see the beautiful Island of Avalon.

**Psalms 72:11** May all kings fall down before him, all nations serve him!

# Chapter Eleven
## Do the Animals still Talk on Christmas Eve?

When I was a little girl, my dad read me the story about the tradition that the animals could talk for a few minutes on Christmas Eve at midnight, when they are supposed to bear witness to the wonder of the first Christmas. I thought everything dad said must be true, and I tried my darndest to stay up until midnight to see if my collie dog Rex would talk. I'd have even settled for hearing from mom's goldfish. My big brother told me it only worked with farm animals; and of course, he was four years older and knew about such things, so I let it drop. I was about five at the time.

When I was nine, we moved to the country. We had all of three and a half acres, and we had two ponies and two beef steers and chickens and two dogs and barn cats. Christmas time came, and I decided to find out for myself if the legend was true or if it was like that Santa Claus story, which my big brother again had put me wise to as being a cover up for getting lots of toys. He advised I act like I believed it. I could read now and I got down the old book of Christmas tales and reread it. It was in a book so it had to be true, yes? For several days after that last blast about Santa from big brother I reasoned this thing out. This idea of the animals talking had to be true; because it had to do with God, and He had to exist, the preacher said so and some grown-up had written it in a book, and Dad had read it to me. I asked my big brother and he suggested I might want to rethink the whole idea of going outside in the dark, cautioning me if mom and dad found out, I'd get a blistered tail instead of presents for

Christmas. I asked him to join me so I wouldn't be alone and he demurred. This was up to me. I started to plan my foray into the midnight snow.

Christmas eve, I was supposed to be in bed waiting for Santa. Dad was in the basement, tending the furnace, he said, but I knew he was putting together bikes, I'd see them hidden behind the furnace in boxes. Mom had gone to bed after putting my little sister, age five and baby brother, age 1 to bed and telling me to head to bed as well. I went upstairs, waited until her bedroom door closed, counted to fifty, and slipped down the stairs.

Putting my coat over my pajamas was the simple part. I got my mom's flashlight, which we were not supposed to touch, out of the kitchen drawer. I went to the back door and quietly undid the bolt lock and the door lock; dad always locked everything at dusk. Pulling the door quietly behind me, I headed down the drive to the big gate on the back field. I opened it, went in, closed it and headed out to the stable.

The back door of the stable was open, and the animals could go in and out; it wasn't really very cold out for them that night. There was a blanket of snow that had fallen over the last couple days to everyone's delight since a white Christmas was a good thing, especially for farmers. The snow made the ground more fertile. It was also really pretty to look at, shiny and sparkly in the moonlight. The moon was at half, so I could see shadows on the snow from the trees, making it just a little bit spooky. I remember blowing out my breath to see it fog in the air. My dog joined me on my amble to the barn. The creek hadn't frozen over yet, and I could hear it burbling along downfield.

I went into the stable side of the barn and shined the flashlight since it was a lot darker in here than outside. The ponies were in one stall, the half-grown steers the other. It was really dark but I turned off the flashlight, because I knew I wasn't supposed to run down the batteries and I really wasn't supposed to have it. I patted the ponies on the nose and explained to them when it was time, they could start by telling me what their horse names actually were; I called them Lark and Midnight but they might have had other names before. I got out some grain from the feed barrel and gave them a treat. They munched contentedly. I yawned.

I sat down on a bale of straw by the feed barrel and waited. And waited. And, you guessed it, I fell asleep.

Now dad got the bikes together finally around midnight and came upstairs. He went up to check on the kids before heading for bed himself. Mike, Cindy, asleep in their beds, baby Tiny in the crib with his thumb in his mouth, fine. Jeanette, not in her bed; not in the bathroom, not with mom. He woke mom up, and now both mom and dad were frantically looking all over, calling out, trying not to wake the other kids, checking the basement, the coal room, in the closets, nothing.

It was mom that discovered the unlocked back door. Dad grabbed his big utility flashlight and headed outside, following my tracks to the stable, where he found me asleep. He shook me.

"Girl, what are you doing out here in the barn? You like to scared your mom and me to death and you could freeze out here."

"Did the animals talk yet?" I yawned. "I want to hear them talk at midnight."

An odd look came over his face as he looked at me. He shook his head. "You slept right through it!" he exclaimed immediately figuring out what I had been doing and not wanting to mess with tradition. "Midnight's come and gone. And if you don't get into the house, you'll miss Santa Claus as well."

He rustled me up and I stumbled my way back to the house by way of the big flashlight he held. I got to the kitchen, put mom's flashlight away and then went to bed, colder and disgruntled over having missed my one chance to talk to the animals. By the next year, I was too big to believe in such things as Santa and talking animals. Older and wiser at ten, I told the tale to my little sister and it was her turn to try and stay awake long enough to go hear the animals. None of us ever did hear them.

It did get me wondering where the legend came from. I traced it back to European legends, that also included the bees singing the angel song at midnight in the hives (and we keep bees and I can vouch they don't hum much in winter), and oxen kneeling in their stalls at the stroke of midnight in honor of the king. The idea was based on the fact the when Jesus, the Creator of all things, was born as a baby, it was such a miraculous event, such a wondrous thing, that all nature reacted, including being able to sing, talk and pray out loud to the Good Lord who had been born in a manger that night in Bethlehem. Centuries of children have wistfully wished it were so, and maybe someday, when the Lord comes back, we will be able to communicate with the animals.

## Colossians 1:16-17

For by Him all things were created that are in heaven and that are on earth, visible and invisible, whether thrones or dominions or principalities or powers. All things were created through Him and for Him. And He is before all things, and in Him all things consist.

# Story Twelve
# Why Do We Hang Mistletoe?

The Bible speaks of a Branch coming; of course, the original Branch from the family of David predicted by Jeremiah was Jesus, who would come, live, die and go back to heaven to be both our judge and defense attorney in the heavenly courts. However, according to Christmas traditions, there is another branch that had to do with good and evil, and that was a small parasitic plant called the mistletoe.

Mistletoe is one of the most sacred and magical plants in folklore. For centuries, the sprigs of mistletoe have been used in Christmas decorations. In Norse folklore, it protects the house from fire and lightening. Another belief in Scandinavian countries is that mistletoe is a plant of peace and friendship; kissing under the mistletoe ensures peace the next year. The idea that a lady standing under the mistletoe cannot refuse to be kissed came into force later in the legends; it was also supposed to be a declaration of love and an invitation to marry. (I suspect most folks forget about that last part today!) Some of the superstitions concerning mistletoe are of pagan origins; some Norse, some Viking, some from druid worship, but let's see how far we've been able to trace them back.

Most mistletoe legends originated in Iceland, from the northern Germanic peoples, and the area of Scandinavia. Their pantheon of Gods included Thor, Frigga, Odin, Loki, and Freya among others. The mistletoe legend about kissing under the plant harks back to the Viking story of Frigga and her son Balder. Frigga was the goddess of love. Her son Balder was the God of the summer sun.

One night, Balder had a nightmare. He called for his mother, who came to him at once as any good mother would do.

"Mother, I had a terrible dream!" he exclaimed. "I saw my death. I saw you weeping. I saw me on the burial mound." Frigga sat down on the edge of his bed.

"My son, tell me more of this dream." She was concerned because the vividness of the dream suggested it might be a prophetic vision. Frigga knew that if Balder died, life on earth would die as well, since he was the sun that made all things on earth live with his light. The death of the earth would herald the approach of Ragnarök and the end of all things.

After hearing Balder out, she told the other gods and after a lot of discussion, they went out all over the planet, requesting and receiving assurances from every living thing, plant, animal, even the ground, rocks, pebbles, fish, nothing would ever harm Balder. Frigga thought she had covered everything and felt he was safe now. The vision could not come true.

But Loki, god of mischief, was an enemy of Balder. Loki wanted the dream to come true. He searched far and wide and realized one little plant had not made a promise to Frigga. That little plant was the lowly mistletoe. A parasite, mistletoe grows up high in oak or apple trees, taking sustenance from what it grows upon. It's such a small plant, no one really noticed it, and Frigga hadn't seen it so it had promised nothing. Loki plucked the plant, fashioned an arrow from it and placed a twig of sharpened mistletoe on its' tip. He took it to his brother, a blind God named Hoder, god of winter, during a feast celebrating how they had changed fate. Everyone had been making great sport of the fact nothing could touch Balder. They tossed stones, cups, knives-everything turned away as if by magic. Loki gave Hoder his special arrow, helped him point it and Hoder, wanting to join in the fun and never dreaming anything bad, shot the arrow in the general direction of his brother. To everyone's horror, it homed in on Balder and struck him dead.

The sun died, and the earth turned brown and frozen. People were starving, life became a misery of cold and dark. All of creation tried to bring Balder back. One younger god even traveled to see Hel, goddess of death, to beg for his return. However, she said for Balder to return, everyone on earth would have to weep for him. The call went out and everyone except a certain giantess (who is said to have been Loki in disguise) wept. Hel attempted to keep Balder, but she was unable to do so because the earth refused to keep him, the gods decreed he had to return. However, due to the one person who would not weep for him, it was decreed by fate that for six months, Hoder would hold sway on the planet and Baldur the other six months, so we have winter and summer. Frigga was so overjoyed to have her son back, she forgave Hoder for his part in the death, and she cried tears of joy which fell on the little mistletoe, changing into white berries which it still bears today. Other cultures adopted mistletoe as special; druids hung it over the door of newly-weds to ensure fertility. In the middle ages, it was thought to have healing properties. Still later in the Victorian era, a man could kiss a girl under the mistletoe, but has to pluck a berry each time, when the berries were gone, so was the liberty to kiss someone.

So what has this all got to do with Christmas and mistletoe? Undoubtedly the idea of resurrection, of evil killing good, but good overcoming evil, bring us to remember the mistletoe. Perhaps the idea of it just being good luck and an excuse to kiss pretty girls during a holiday party makes us think of it at Christmas. Perhaps the thing to remember is that the true Branch has come among us and is with us, and someday, will return to bring us to a place of perfect peace and happiness.

Jeremiah 23:5

"Behold, *the* days are coming," says the Lord, "That I will raise to David a Branch of righteousness; A King shall reign and prosper, and execute judgment and righteousness in the earth.

# Story Thirteen
# Poinsettias, the Gift from Mexico

Dr. Joel Poinsett was the first ambassador to Mexico in 1823. He fell in love with the lovely poinsettia plants growing wild there. As an amateur botanist with greenhouses back home in North Carolina, and having talked to the natives about the plant's healing properties, he sent some back to be cultivated at home. In Central America and Mexico, the flower is also known as 'Flame Leaf' or 'Flower of the Holy Night'.

The legend related to this favorite Christmas flower is Mexican and we will get to it in a moment. The ancient Aztecs used the plant as a medicinal herb and as a fabric dye, not red dye, oddly enough, but more of a purplish- pink color. It can grow up to twelve feet tall. When I have visited in the southern part of the United States, I have seen bushes almost that large growing in yards. There are over 34 million poinsettias sold at Christmas and we have hybridized them to have huge bracts, in shades of red, white, green, pink and purple-even dying them blue.

What I find most interesting is that the true flower part of the poinsettia is the tiny yellow parts in the center-the rest is actually another form of leaf, called bracts. I remember working in a greenhouse concern in Maine and being amazed by the houses of poinsettias we grew each year, literally thousands of them, grown, sold and delivered each December. The plant now grows in different colors and folks can pick the one that matches their décor at home, be it straight or curly bracts, in shades of white, pink, purple-even dyed blue!

So how did the poinsettia get tied to Christmas traditions? It's a Mexican story.

However, there are two versions of the story. In the first version, the two small children of the story are called Maria and her little brother Pablo; while in another version, two cousins are mentioned called Pepita and Pedro. We know there were two children, that doesn't change, so we'll use Maria and Pedro to give a nod to each version.

Once upon a time, Maria and Pedro, a little boy and girl, lived with their family. They were terribly poor. Life was a big struggle. They lived in a village and although they tried hard, it was often difficult to get just one meal a day.

As in all the villages in Mexico, as the Christmas season approached, the village was filled with peddlers and parties, parades and festivities. The children were attracted to the fun, but with wistful hearts for the parties and candy, baked goods and festivals had no place for those who could not pay. The gaiety of the season in itself was all around and the children could not help but hear about the gifts that were going to be brought to the Christ child. The church had set up a large manger scene. All the children were encouraged to bring the baby Jesus a special present for his birthday on Christmas eve.

Maria and Pedro wanted to give gifts to the Holy Child for his birthday, but they had nothing. While all the other children were discussing among themselves what they were going to bring and how they would buy the gifts, Maria and Pedro knew there would be no gifts from them. They discussed maybe giving their tortilla that day as a gift; but their mother said no, they had to eat to be healthy. Mother assured them that any gift they made for Jesus if given in love, the Christ child would accept; while in her heart, she wept for her children's sadness, but could do nothing.

She thought perhaps it would be best not to attend mass that Christmas eve, so they would not have to go without a gift. But the children could not let go of the temptation to see the Baby just once – He only came once a year to the church. It would be a whole year before He came again. On Christmas Eve, Maria and Pedro set out for church a little earlier than others to attend the service. Since they had nothing to give to the child, they thought of plucking some dry grass and weeds that was growing along the roadside to put in the manger to make a soft bed for him to lie on. They slept on grass and straw; would not the Baby Jesus feel better had he a sweet-smelling mat of grass? They could do that. They scurried about, gathering the softest, longest weeds and grass they could find until they had quite bundle and tied it together, arriving earlier than the other children so they could fill the manger making a soft bed for Baby Jesus.

While they were still arranging the crib for the Baby, other children also arrived. Children can be very cruel when it comes to teasing and making fun of others not so fortunate as themselves. Mario and Pedro were almost in tears for shame and helplessness when it happened. The straw they had gathered suddenly burst into bright red petals that looked like stars and were so beautiful that everyone was in awe. The people realized they had just seen a miracle; a gift from the Father above and His son. They saw the wonderful flowers and they finally realized that a gift of love is dearer to Jesus than the most expensive presents that money could buy. Ever since then, Poinsettia flowers have been a part of Christmas and they remind us that love is the spirit of Christmas, love, sacrifice and beauty.

61

"Christmas is like candy; it slowly melts in your mouth sweetening every taste bud, making you wish it could last forever." – *Richelle E. Goodrich*

# Story Fourteen

# The Morning and Evening Stars sang Together

Once upon a time, two thousand years plus a few years for practice, there were two angels who lived in the heavenly courts. One was a morning star and wore bright pink and lavender robes; she sang in a lovely soprano voice and was called Anael. Her angel friends called her Annie. Her best friend was an evening star, and he wore dark blue and gold streaked robes, and he sane baritone in the heavenly chorus. His name was Englebert; she called him Bert. Their days were filled with morning chorus, joint chorus around the throne at mid-day and evening chorus towards evening. They sang marvelous duets about the love of God prepared for them by their angelic choir leader. They often used to take turns leading the angel orchestra and chorus, as did all their musical friends.

One day their orchestra leader and director of music came winging into choir practice with exciting news.

"Angels, gather round!" he shouted. "You will not believe what's happening down on that poor, old, dark earth!"

The angels came closer and listened, lying down their music sheets.

"The Lord God just told Gabriel and Gabriel told me, that something wonderful is going to happen," he proclaimed. "Jesus, the only begotten Son, is going to go to earth to save the world from the evil."

"Will he be leading the angel armies?" asked Englebert. "I'd like to see that."

"No, he'll be going in disguise."

"Disguise?" asked another angel.

"Yes, he has to wrap his majesty in a form they will accept down there. He's going to go to earth as a human baby."

"A baby!" gasped the chorus.

'One of those little humans who can't talk, can't walk, spits up, burps, messes themselves and is pretty well useless for the first dozen years or so? That sort of baby?" asked Annie.

"Exactly." said the director. "He's going to go as a baby because no one is afraid of babies. You know yourselves, some of you who have been messengers, the first thing a human does when they see one of us is go all boggly eyed and nearly die of fright. No one could be afraid of such a little one. He is going to be born shortly in a town named Bethlehem. And we're going to go sing to him and to some very special shepherds. Now we need to practice this new piece. It's called Glory to God in the Highest, and on earth peace, good will towards men."

Both Engelbert and Annie played heavenly silver trumpets in the orchestra, besides singing. They saw there was a line for trumpeting in the music, and they prepared their instruments. The new piece called for everyone in the joint orchestra and chorus to perform in a magical, inspirational, magnificent chorus, wearing their brightest robes and floating just above the earth. It would be the jubilee performance of their lives, announcing the birth of God's King.

It wasn't until a few days later, that the angel director explained they'd be in the skies over Bethlehem singing to fifteen or twenty shepherds and their sheep.

"Shepherds?" asked Annie.

"Sheep?" echoed Bert.

"Yes, we're going to tell them where to go see their new Lord and from them the word will grow and spread that He has arrived. Now let's go over page five again."

Shortly after, as they were practicing, the angel Gabriel came bustling in, dressed in his finest robes, carrying a scroll.
"It's time!" he announced. "The baby is being born as I speak and we need to get to the fields above Bethlehem at once."
The angel choir and orchestra joined him in the air and they streaked at faster than the speed of light to Bethlehem. Gabriel led them to a field surrounded by hills, where a campfire was burning in the chilly evening.

The angel choir and the orchestra waited for the signal and when given, flung off the cloak of darkness and floated in the sky, emblazoned across it; then they began to sing,

"Glory to God in the Highest and on earth, good will, goodwill towards men"

The piece went on for five minutes, growing more magnificent, stronger and louder, ending in a crescendo of sound followed by profound silence as it stopped. Then Gabriel stepped in front of the choir and announced from his scroll:

"Rejoice! Do not be afraid! For there is born this day in the city of David a Savior, who is Christ the Lord. You will find the babe dressed in swaddling clothes and lying in a manger. Go and give worship to Him."

He held their eyes for a moment, those poor shepherds lying on the ground, staring up in shock. Then suddenly, the entire heavenly chorus just winked out. They were there, and then it was ever so dark. As the shepherds shook their heads in amazement and looked around, blinking and whispering, their leader finally said "Let's go on up and see if we can find a baby lying in a manger. After all, heaven sends all those angels, and I don't think I was seeing something that wasn't there, it's time to move." and they all headed to Bethlehem.

Meanwhile, here we are, two thousand years later, and we are looking back to the angels and their wonderful songs. One of my musical friends tells me that he thinks the chorus Glory to God from the Messiah must have been very much like what was sung, God inspiring Handel, wanting it to echo again down through the generations and he'd waited all that time to find someone who could do it justice. I don't know. But at Christmas time, we have angels seemingly everywhere as one of the great symbols of Christmas.

And Annie and Bert? I imagine they're still in heaven, waiting to come to earth singing yet another song of triumph when The Lord returns to take us all back home.

When the morning stars sang together,
And all the sons of God shouted for joy? Job 38:7

# Story Fifteen
# The Christ-child Visits the Earth

There is a belief in many old world countries that on Christmas
Eve, the Christ child comes once again to earth to see if anyone
will be kind to Him, sort of like hoping that when He came the
first time, He made a difference in our lives. He visits people in
disguise and sees if they will help a lonely stranger. This is one
such retelling of that story. Some say this belief is what led to
the decorating of the Christmas tree; others that it is a way to
help us remember what the season actually is about-care and
love and help for others.

Once upon a time, there was a poor woodcutter who worked
hard all year to make enough money to support his family.
There were three in his family, himself, his wife and his two
children Michael and Marie. All of the family worked to help
provide food for the table and keep the roof over their heads.
Father cut the wood, his son and daughter stacked it into a
wagon; the mother cooked and cleaned and helped stack the
wood in long rows to dry when they got it back to the cabin.
Much of their wood was sold in the fall, after it had been drying
so it would be good firewood. Little Marie gathered all the
wood chips and small branches and made a pile of kindling and
starters with it that they sold by the bucketful. They worked
every day except the Sabbath; on that day they made sure their
home was clean, they put on their best clothing and they went to
church. They were a pious family, they read their Bible every
morning before setting out for work; they prayed together each

night. Most of all, they were content and happy with their life, though simple, it was good.

The winter was hard that year and it came early. Father had stacked his sled with wood, tied their pony to it and they had both set off to make deliveries before snowfall. Mother and the children had prepared the next load for Father to save him time, they made soup and bread, swept their little house clean. The next day was Christmas and they hoped to make the day a festive one if they could. Michael and Marie did not know that mother had knitted them warm mittens, or that father had carved a wooden horse for Michael and built a small wooden bed for Mary's dolly. Mother had made some small honey cakes for Christmas dinner.

During the long morning, there came a knock at the window. Marie looked out and cried, "Mother, look. A poor child is outside on our doorstep!"

Mother came, opened the door and they ushered the little child in. His feet were wrapped in rags, he was thin and shivering and suffering. Marie took him to the fire and settled him down by the fire. Mother fetched him a bowl of soup and a piece of warm bread, Michael rubbed his feet until they were warm again. He seemed so tired. They made a bed up for him by the fire.

"What's this?" asked Father when he came home. "I don't remember a third child."

"Shh," replied Mother. "He came to our door, cold and hungry and we put him here to keep him warm. He can stay through

Christmas then we will need to take him into the church to see if anyone is missing a child."

"Who would send a child out without even a blanket in weather like this?" asked Father, reaching down and pushing the hair from the little boy's face. "A handsome child he is, but so thin. You fed him?"

"Yes, dear, and now it is time for us to have our soup as well. The bread is still warm from the fire, and the soup is good. I made some little cookies for special since this is Christmas Eve."

"It's blustery out, and it was all I could do to get home," Father replied after they had said grace. "Twill be first Christmas in a long time we do not go to the service down in the village. I would not risk the children, though, and the pastor said when I delivered him wood, that he had told everyone to stay home. There is a blizzard coming in. If it clears, in the morning he will ring the bells and we shall go in to the service."

"I suppose the little boy can come with us then," sighed the Mother. "I did not get his name. He did not speak overmuch except to say thank you."

"I've already bedded the pony for the night and gave her an extra hand of grain for her hard work this day. I brought in the eggs; there were five."
"The cold is stopping the hens from laying," replied Mother. "But the garden was good this year. If we are frugal, we should make it through until spring."

"God is good," answered her husband.

The child slept on. In their prayers that night, they asked the Good Lord to be kind to the little boy and find him a good home, if he had none. They all went to their beds and father banked the fire to keep it going; mother set bread dough on the table to raise for the next day. Soon all that could be heard was the sound of the wind howling, the swishing of the snow falling and drifting, the soft sounds of a family snuggled in for a long winter night.

At dawn, they were woken by the sounds of music playing and light. The music could be heard above the storm, harps and bells and soft singing.

"Children, it must be the angels singing to the Christ child, born last night. Dress quickly, quickly!" The family went down the ladder and ran to a window where, through the storm, they could see a number of angels singing, playing harps, and a holy light that seeming to burn through the blizzard. Turning around, they realized the little boy was gone; his ragged clothing was folded neatly and sat by the fire along with the blanket and pillow.

There was a knock on the door and Father opened it with no little bit of fear in his heart. The little boy from last night was now dressed in white robes, with a crown on his head. He smiled at them.

"You showed me kindness last night, as I wandered the earth looking for people of good heart and kindness. I came to your door and you let me in, you fed me, you made me warm, you gave me a place to sleep. I have this for your kindness."

He held in his hand the bough of a tree. He took it outside and stuck it in the ground where it took root and grew to a good height, shielding their little house from the storm winds. He touched its' branches and it was covered with golden apples and silvered nuts, toys and tools they needed, candies in little bags.

"Gather ye the fruit of your kindness," smiled the Christ child. "The tree is here for you to each year decorate and remember me. May my Father bless you always." Suddenly the angels and the Child were gone. The family gathered the food and gifts off the tree and brought them inside, where added to the mittens mother had knitted, and the food they had prepared, made a feast they had never had before. When Father went out to feed his pony and their hens, he found their feed barrels filled to the brim with grain, the hayloft full of hay. He looked at his woodpile to be sold and found it had doubled overnight.

In the house, the mother found her flour barrel full, her salt jar full, a two extra baskets of dried beans and more jars of honey than she knew she had before. Their blankets seemed thicker, their home warmer and they knew in their hearts, best of all, that they had pleased the Lord.

**Matthew 25: 37-40** Then the righteous will answer Him, saying, 'Lord, when did we see You hungry and feed *You,* or thirsty and give *You* drink? When did we see You a stranger and take *You* in, or naked and clothe *You?* Or when did we see You sick, or in prison, and come to You?' And the King will answer and say to them, 'Assuredly, I say to you, inasmuch as you did *it* to one of the least of these My brethren, you did *it* to Me.'

# Day Sixteen
## The Year the Goats put out the Lights...

Nativities, representations of the night Jesus was born, have always held a fascination for me. I really a small set my mother used to put out each year for Christmas, and other sets we used through the years. At present we have a beautiful porcelain set that we put out each year.

The history of the use of nativities in churches and homes as a decoration and a point of remembrance dates back to St. Francis of Assisi in 1223 who was trying to get the worship part of Christmas back into Christmas; he was dismayed at the commercialism of the celebration of Christmas, the extravagance, the neglect of the poor. He thought having a scene representing the birth of the Christ would be a reminder of what the season really was about. (Sound familiar to anyone?) Nearly eight hundred years ago, they had the same problems with commercialization we do today! Some things don't change.

However, I do remember the year of the live nativity, an event that happened when we were young parents. Our church was casting about to make a different sort of Christmas program than the usual pageant. Since many of us had kids, it was a big event at our small church.

Our family had just acquired some goats, another lady had donkeys, still another sheep, well, it sort of snowballed and you get the idea. Harry and John and friends built us a stable we put in the lower parking area. The ladies made costumes; the performers were chosen. Dan, Robin and I went over and set up cow panels to hold the various animals: by now we had angora rabbits, chickens, pigeons, two sheep, three goats, a cow, a donkey, a pony, a dog, two cats, one rather large and amiable grey goose and a guinea pig. I don't know how the guinea pig got there.

At any rate, the petting zoo that was assembled was pretty amazing. My oldest daughter, a shy girl of fifteen, was to be Mary. The night we performed our living nativity was cold and clear, the cherub choir was ever so cute in their white robes over snowsuits and somewhat bent tinsel halos, the live baby we had was actually six months old and slept like the proverbial angel. Dan had hung multicolored lights all over the front of the stable, we had a small manger filled with hay, lots of straw bales around the family. We had lots of visitors. Cue the music, what could go wrong?

The shepherds took their job too seriously. They had costumes, crooks, and six-year-old inventive imaginations and thought it would look good to have the animals in the nativity with the rest the people, not in the pens. They let first the sheep out, then the goats and the chickens. Stopped in their mischief, we had to chase down the sheep and get them back first, then locate the goats who were rapidly eating the electric light bulbs. I kid you not, the goats were coiling in lights like candy. Cornered and caught again, they went back to their pen under some duress. When a billy goat is under duress, you know what he does? He pees on his face. Seriously. It's really nasty. The chickens had roosted on the top of the stable and we couldn't convince them to come down. The donkey, who was normally docile, didn't like being led by the wise men along with the pony and kept trying to bite him. Turns out, Smaller Wise men are scared of leading real animals. Bigger, not in costume, Wise men had to separate the animals and walk them around to calm them down.

To draw attention from the chaos in the petting zoo, the folks showing off the animals invited everyone to go over by the manger where Dan had hung more lights, so they could actually watch the little performance, the kids reciting their lines. The angels began their song again, the local newspaper took pictures, Mary prodded Joseph into talking louder by kicking him quietly behind the manger. The Baby peacefully slept through everything and the narrator managed to get his lines out in spite of the public address system shorting out from being chewed by the rabbits who had somehow pulled the wire inside their cage. In a little over two hours, it was done for the year, we all went inside to have hot cocoa and homemade cookies.

It all happened thirty years ago, but has gone down in our family's history as the year the goats ate the lights...our pastor at the time, a very good man, had blessedly been visiting the sick at the hospital and got there just in time to see us load up the animals.
I sincerely hope St. Francis had a better time of it.

Matthew 1:21. And she shall bring forth a son, and thou shalt call his name Jesus: for he shall save his people from their sins.

# Day Seventeen
# Why Do we Get Oranges in our Stockings?

I suppose the first thing to establish is why stockings at all? In the old stories about Saint Nicholas, we find he was a church leader with a huge heart. He helped others whenever and where ever he could. One Advent, in his parish was a man who had three daughters. Now back in those days, when a woman got married, the family had to provide a dowry, a sum of money supposed to help get the new family established. If something happened to her husband, or if he reneged on his vows, the money was supposed to help her in supporting herself. This particular family was poor, and without a dowry, the girls could not be married and the father could not afford to keep them, so would have to sell them into slavery.

Good Saint Nicholas heard about the girls' plight and thought about it. He knew that each night the girls, as all people in that land, washed their socks and hung them by the fire to dry. Under cover of darkness, he put small pouches of gold in each of their stockings, enough for a dowry. The girls were able to marry and not become someone's slave. From that day to this, we put stockings out Christmas Eve so Santa (St. Nicholas) can put gifts in them.

Now back to the orange.

During the depression, oranges were often the only gift a poor family could get for their children. Oranges were somewhat exotic, they were pretty, and something you didn't see every day. My own father remembered each Christmas an orange was put in his stocking and those of his siblings, followed by hard candy, nuts to crack and if they were very lucky that year, some small toy. He remembered one year they'd all gone to bed without supper, they simply didn't have enough food in the house to have three meals and being a growing boy, he was really hungry. He got up in the middle of the night, crept into the kitchen and ate the entire bag of oranges. I remember him telling us all this story when we were kids; the last time I can remember him telling it, he was 83. He says he still remembered the whipping he got the next morning; but most of all, he remembered the disappointment on his sister's faces as they missed their orange that year. His brothers waited until he got upstairs and pummeled him for good measure. Treats didn't come easily during the depression. He had no breakfast that day, nor lunch or any of the nuts or candy the others had but was allowed to come out of his room for dinner. He remembered they had chicken and noodles for dinner. He would always end with saying, "And that's how I learned not to steal, no matter how hungry I was."

Oranges represented hope to the people crippled by the depression. They represented belief that tomorrow could be better, the country would not fall, and someday, everyone would have a job and food and firewood or coal again and good clothes. Today might be cold and hard, but tomorrow was coming.

**John 10:27-28**
My sheep listen to my voice; I know them, and they follow me. I give them eternal life, and they will never perish. No one can snatch them away from me.

# Day Eighteen

## One more time: Oh, Christmas Tree, Oh, Christmas Tree...

It has been said that the Christmas tree, with its evergreen branches represents the eternal love God has for everyone in the world, a love that does not change. The lights on the tree tell us that Jesus is the light of the world. Martin Luther, the father of the reformation, cut the first Christmas tree in 1535 and put it in his house for his children who decorated it. Later on, Prince Albert of England learned of the German tradition and brought a Christmas tree into Windsor castle in 1841. In 1851, a minister in Cleveland Ohio was accused of sacrilege when he put the first tree up in a church he headed. The beauty and grace of the tree, it's fragrance and welcome, soon had people copying the idea and putting trees in their own homes.

But back before all this history was occurring, how did we choose an evergreen for a tree to represent Christ? There's not exactly Scripture for it. This is the story as it was told to me.

Two thousand years ago, when Jesus was born, everyone was very happy, the Shepherds, the wise men, the angels, the children, the animals, birds and nature itself. Jesus was born to bring salvation, peace between us and God and each other. People gave the baby gifts to celebrate His birth. People came daily to see the little One, (just like today, everyone wants to hold the baby) and they always brought gifts with them. Now there were three trees growing by the cave stable. They wished they could give gifts to the Child as well, but what can a tree give?

The Palm tree, growing down the hill a little way promised: "I will choose my most beautiful leaf, and place it as a fan over the Child. Later in his life, I will wave as he enters Jerusalem to be crowned King."

"And I," said the Olive, "will provide sweet-smelling oil upon His head and to keep his skin soft and healthy."

"What can I give to the Child?" asked the Fir, who stood near, bending just such a little bit to look back into the cave.

And the other trees cried out in horror. "You? You have nothing! Your needles would prick Him, and your sap is so sticky. Stay back, don't harm the babe."

The poor little Fir tree was very unhappy as it considered what the others said: "They're right. I would be a danger to the child. I have nothing to offer." His branches drooped.

The trees did not notice that near them stood the Christmas Angel, and he had overheard everything they said. The Angel was sorry for the Fir tree who really was a good little tree, and had only wanted to bring his Creator honor. The angel looked up to Creator with a silent request. He nodded and looked back. The Father had sent a few of the little stars of heaven to come down and rest upon the branches of the Fir tree and it shone suddenly with a beautiful light.

And, at that very moment, the Christ Child opened His eyes and as the lovely light fell upon Him He smiled.

And every year, people put up Christmas trees and give gifts to each other in honor of that Holy night. The evergreen trees,

covered in lights and ornaments in remembrance of the first
Christmas eve, shine and shimmer and dance in children's eyes,
as that first tree must have made the baby Jesus glad as well.
For our Lord loves to make His people happy. All around the
world, where ever Christmas is kept, the Christmas tree is a
wish for us to come closer to Him who made us, restored and
saved us, and wishes us all love and peace.


"Christmas waves a magic wand over this world, and behold,
everything is softer and more beautiful." – *Norman Vincent
Peale*

# Day Nineteen
# Why did my True Love Bring to me all that Stuff?

I think everyone has heard the Song called the Twelve Days of Christmas, but did you know it had a historic, hidden meaning?

From 1558 until 1829, it was illegal to be Catholic in England. As the historical line goes, someone in France, history has lost their name, made up this little song with twelve imaginative ways for Catholic parents to help their children learn their catechism. One historian notes that the gifts, added up together, total 364-the days in a year minus Christmas. According to this line of thinking, the meaning of the verses is this:

On the first day of Christmas, **my true love** (God in heaven) gave to **me** (every baptized believer in the world): (I simply list the gifts and meanings so as not to keep repeating myself)

*a partridge in a pear tree*- baby Jesus whom God gave to the world on the first day of Christmas.
*two turtle doves* – the Old and New Testaments that comprise *the Bible*
*three French hens* -Faith, Hope and Love, listed at the end of I Corinthians 13 as what abides after all else is gone.
*Four Calling birds* – the four Gospels, Matthew Mark Luke and John
five golden rings – The Torah, the first five books of the Bible
*six geese alaying*– six days of creation
*seven maids amilking* -the seven sacraments (Baptism, Eucharist/Communion, Confirmation, Reconcilition, Annointing of the Sick, Marriage and Holy Orders)
*eight swans a swimming*-the eight beatitudes (I've listed them below)

*nine Ladies dancing*- Nine fruits of the Holy Spirit (love, joy, peace, patience, goodness, forbearance, gentleness, faith, self-control
*ten Lords a leaping* – The Ten Commandments
*eleven pipers piping* – eleven apostles without Judas
*twelve drummers drumming*- Twelve points in the Apostles' creed

Later, the tune was so lively and the words seemed so nicely commercial (what's not to like about getting presents each day?) that it got to be very popular in England and was brought here by English immigrants. Someone added up the costs of all those hens and swans and decided were someone to do this today, it would cost them $40,000. It is a joke of our ancestors that what was once a mnemonic device to help children learn their Bible lessons became a secular Christmas song.

*"Blessed are the poor in spirit, for theirs is the kingdom of heaven.*
*Blessed are they who mourn, for they shall be comforted.*
*Blessed are the meek, for they shall inherit the earth.*
*Blessed are they who hunger and thirst for righteousness, for they shall be satisfied.*
*Blessed are the merciful, for they shall obtain mercy.*
*Blessed are the pure of heart, for they shall see God.*
*Blessed are the peacemakers, for they shall be called children of God.*
*Blessed are they who are persecuted for the sake of righteousness,*
*for theirs is the kingdom of heaven." Matthew 5:3-10*

# Day Twenty
# The Dark Side of Christmas Fables...

There's a song goes round this time of year called "It's the Most Wonderful Time of the Year," and one line always caught my ear and held on. The line is: "They'll be scary ghost stories and tales of the glories of Christmases long time ago". Why on earth would anyone tell scary stories at Christmas? Wasn't Herod bad enough to think about? It appears not. In many traditions, we have scary things happening around this time of year. (You might also ponder the fact that one of the most famous and well-known Christmas stories is Dickens' A Christmas Carol- about ghosts past, present and future.) The Victorians ate this stuff up, and it isn't the only story written about Christmas that can make the hair on your neck lift a bit as you read it.

However, I'd like to look at some other countries and the bogymen of Christmas...you would be surprised at the creepiness we've added to the tale of the Christ-child, I think. Most of the stories were most likely used to keep rowdy little kids in line as they got cabin fever from not being able to go out and run. Santa Claus was the good guy rewarding the good little children, but these figures don't come from the North Pole or anything like it. Let's just take a short look.

Our first strange person hails from Germany and is called Belsnickel. "Bels" means "fur" in German and nickel here refers to jolly old St. Nicholas, so Belsnickel is St. Nick in furs or pelts. He actually does hand out a snack or two to extremely good children. However, while Santa is all red and white and shiny black boots, Belsnickle is grimy and smelly and outright dirty. He carries switches in his bag along with candy and nuts and if you are a bad child, you get a whipping instead of a treat.

**La Befana is** Italian. She is portrayed as looking like a haggard old lady, but she really isn't that bad. She has a good heart. She is actually a witch. Yes, a witch. When the Wise men arrived to gift the baby Jesus and worship, she wanted to join them as they traveled but she had so much work to do and they didn't wait, and she had to leave later. Trying so hard to catch up, she threw herself under a tree to rest and a branch fell off the tree, turned into a magical broomstick and she flew around, looking for the baby Jesus. She arrives sometime during epiphany but by that time, baby Jesus has left the stable. Today, although she looks like a witch, she hands out candy and goodies to children and reminds them not to get so hard working they miss what's important.

**Grýla** comes from Iceland. She eats bad children. At Christmas, when the days are shorter and nights longer and darker, she comes down from her mountain cave, looking for bad little children. With her horns and tails and warts, she is a truly hideous, scary figure. She gathers all the bad children in her sack and goes back up mountain and makes stew out of them. In Iceland, they threaten their children with having to wait outside on Christmas eve and wait for Grýla. If being good for Santa doesn't help you reform, Grýla might just do the trick.

The **Krampus** comes from central European traditions. We think he is actually pre-Christian in his origins. His name comes from the German word Krampen, which means claw. Since

Krampus is a demonic looking figure with claws and horns and a long sticky tongue, that's a pretty good name for him. He hauls off naughty children in his sack and eats them. (Is there a pattern here?)

Nowadays, people celebrate Krampus with parties and carnivals just before Christmas, dressing up in terrible costumes. The idea given is to balance the very sweet, loving traditions of Christmas with a bad tradition sort of like a yin/yang idea. It is supposed to make the peace of Christmas seem sweeter and more loving. I mean, at least your family didn't give you to a monster to get eaten before Christmas, right? There is the Saint of Christmas and the devil of Christmas in their minds. Personally, I could do without the devil part.

Iceland invents the best monsters: maybe because of the long winter nights. However, the **Yule Cat,** known as the **jólakötturinn** in its native Iceland, is very interested in how things look. He towers over the houses, peeking into the windows, looking to see if the children got some new clothes for the next year. If they did, fine, but if they didn't, it figures no one will miss this child and eats them up. So in Iceland, you are guaranteed to get some new article of clothing each year. Maybe don't complain about the new sweater or socks Aunt Sarah sent you; she just saved you from the Yule Cat, a fashionable feline.

Out of the long list of Christmas monsters, the last one we've chosen is from Wales. Called **Mari Lwyd**, this is a skeleton horse. During the holidays of Christmas, partygoers will enter your home carrying a decorated horse skull. The visitors will engage the homeowner with a battle of wit; tossing back and forth insults and one liners, funny poems and sayings. If you decide they're funny enough, you invite them in for refreshments and while they are there, the horse spirit will chase away bad feelings, thoughts and harmful spirits. Many folks invite them in even if their jokes and insults aren't up to par, simply because they want the good luck that comes with hosting the troupe. If they don't come in, your home may be plagued with bad luck in the coming year. What has this got to do with Christmas? In Wales, it's the time of new beginnings and you want the new year to go well, and the home to be safe for the visit of the Christ child so you entertain a group of bores-it might just have been the origin of the office party.

There you have six of the nasties of Christmas; in almost every culture there are one or two bad guys who come around once a year. Whether invented to keep children in line, or invite good instead of evil, we seem to have a penchant for scariness. I heard a professor once say that deep within our psyches, we have an archetype of good/evil and a need to be scared, so we invent monsters. However, the only monster in the original story was Herod; he was bad enough to put all these made up monsters to shame. So why talk about monsters on this happiest time of the year?

Because not all people are happy. As a therapist, I see people all the time who are hurting, sad, lonely; who have no good memories of Christmas. One man told me Christmas was when his dad would go on a three-day bender and they had to shut up and hide. Another lady told me Christmas was when she would be kicked out so no one would have to buy her anything. She'd sleep under a bridge or two until she made it to her grandma's across the county on foot. She'd stay there for a few weeks until it was safe to go home. Not all people have fond memories.

What better way for the evil in the world to twist and destroy something good like the birth of the Babe than by inspiring monster tales to frighten children into obedience? To cause pain where there should not be pain; to inflict suffering where it should not exist. A friend of mine told me she mourns that her children were never able to be really innocent; from the moment they entered the world, it seems social media, schools, even churches work to help kids see the bad side, to break down the naivete of youth and make them cynical and hard. She remembers her youth, playing on a farm, catching fireflies, taking time to lie down and watch clouds. No constant sports lessons or tutoring or anything; just time to use her imagination and curiosity. Is any wonder that children have trouble visualizing the last time they actually felt safe playing outside?

In the twists that are the monsters in the Christmas story, we see a little bit of the cynicism and hardness; unwanted children without new clothes get eaten; bad children get tossed in a sack and made into soup. It must make the angels weep to see and hear how much influence evil has become across the globe. How much then do we need that baby in a manger still; and how much we need the reason He came. Is anyone afraid of a baby? That's why he came the way he did: he didn't bring sidekicks that eat children; he brought angels and lambs, kind people with gifts. True, even back then the devil tried to twist the joy with the murderous Herod; but that was Herod's choice, not God's. God wanted the Silent Night, the angel's song, the animals resting. I think we all want that too.

And she gave birth to her firstborn son and wrapped him in swaddling clothes and laid him in a manger, because there was no place for them in the inn. **Luke 2:7**

# Day Twenty-One

## The Many Dates of Christmas

The traditional Christmas calendar was crowded with dates to observe. In our modern, hurry up age, we've got it down to one day, or if we are lucky, we might take Christmas eve off to finish wrapping gifts, but in the earlier traditions, there were a lot more. Let's look at them.

The four Sundays leading up to Christmas are called Advent, a time of reflection on the season to come. In some churches, we still light Advent candles each Sabbath preceding the birth of Christ.

Christmas celebrations started on Christmas Day and lasted for 12 Days in most traditions so they were known as The 12 Days of Christmas! The traditional twelve days ended on January 5 and were a time of feasting and fun. The British royalty especially had huge festivals and handed out bread and pennies to the populace.

The day after this is called Epiphany, January 6. This is the time that the Wise men are remembered and it corresponds also to the time Jesus was baptized by John as an adult. You are also supposed to take down your Christmas decorations. Some folks leave them up until Candlemas (and some just leave them up forever, it seems, at least in my neighborhood.) Candlemas ends the Christmas season. It occurs 40 days after Christmas; it being the traditional day Christ was circumcised, presented at the temple and prophesied over by Anna and Simeon. It's a very important day in some Orthodox and Catholic churches.

The name Candlemas comes from 'Candle Mass' because in many Candlemas services, the candles are blessed to be used in churches during the coming year or are given out to people for them to use in their homes and private prayers.

In many churches it is a time to forgive each other and go from the church with a renewed spirit of kindness. An all-night vigil is held the night before in some faiths before the candle blessing.

Somehow in America, we've been cheated somehow of some of the meaningful dates for Christmas; perhaps that's why it's become so commercial and concentrated; we've lost the ability to take time and contemplate the entire season, all that happened in the first forty days of Christ's life. Forty seems to have been a frequently used time His life, he fasted for forty days in the wilderness, there were forty days between the Resurrection and the Ascension-so perhaps in our rush to get through the holidays, we're missing out.  Would it do us good to spend a quiet time each of the forty days of Christmas and contemplate His gift to us?

The true light, which gives light to everyone, was coming into the world.  He was in the world, and the world was made through him, yet the world did not know him.  He came to his own, and his own people did not receive him. But to all who did receive him, who believed in his name, he gave the right to become children of God, who were born, not of blood  nor of the will of the flesh nor of the will of man, but of God. And the Word became flesh and dwelt among us, and we have seen his glory, glory as of the only Son from the Father, full of grace and truth. John 1:9-14

# Day Twenty-Two
# Chrismons

Chrismons are Christmas decorations with Christian symbols painted or printed on them. Very often they are used on Christmas trees in churches or in people's homes to remind them there is a "reason for the season."

Chrismons were created in Danville, Virginia by Francis Kipps Spencer and gave them their name. Her idea quickly spread to other churches in the area and then all over, especially in the Lutheran church in the U.S. When she thought of the name, she combined Christmas with monogram-Chrismons. She thought of them as a way to keep God's initials in the celebration. The Chrismons, the traditional ones, are used to tell the story of the birth of Jesus and what happened afterwards.

Chrismons are traditionally colored white and gold. White is the liturgical (or Church) color for Christmas and symbolizes that Jesus was pure and perfect. Gold symbolizes His Majesty and Glory. They can be made of paper, plastic, wood, clay-even as cookies with edible glitter applied. In many churches and families who use them, often the elementary class children make them out of white poster board and hang them on trees in their rooms.

The original thirty-three Chrismons included among them several crosses, (Irish, Latin, triumphant) a lamb, a lion, a crown, a fish, stars, Alpha/Omega, and a manger. You can download patterns to make your own by simply typing in Chrismons, printable patterns into your search engine, then choosing the set that you and you children (if you have any around) would enjoy decorating and hanging on your tree this year. It's a nice way to remember the true meaning behind the symbols of Christmas.

**Matthew 1:23** "Behold, the virgin shall conceive and bear a son, and they shall call his name Immanuel" (which means, God with us).

# Day Twenty-Three

## Building a Tradition of Kindness

One of the many traditions of Christmas is to be kind towards others and in many families, this includes the tradition of being a Secret Santa. If you're going to do this, you locate someone in your neighborhood or your office or church who seems down and sad this season. You target them for extra kindness. As a therapist, I can tell you that you are never so happy as when you are doing something for others without expecting anything in return. Let me give you a couple examples from my own life, not to make me look good, but to give you some ideas on how this could work for you.

Years ago, I worked in an office where there was a lot of stress, simply due to the work we did. I noticed that folks got more stressed and grumpier, more tired and frustrated as the weeks to the holidays started. I got together with a couple of my other friends and set up a plan. One of them made great candy; one liked to bake; I was really into humor. We set up a schedule and on differing days, we'd take in and set up in the break room a plate of home-made candy or cookies; or I'd paper bomb the office doors (tastefully, of course) with funny sayings before anyone got there for work-(Individual mottos, printed on bright paper,) things like

"If a cluttered desk is a sign of a cluttered mind, of what, then, is an empty desk a sign?" – Albert Einstein

"If a book about failures doesn't sell, is it a success?" – Jerry Seinfeld

"Do not take life too seriously, you will never get out of it alive." – Elbert Hubbard

"Before you criticize someone, walk a mile in their shoes. That way, you'll be a mile from them, and you'll have their shoes." – Jack Handey

"Women and cats will do as they please, and men and dogs should relax and get used to the idea." – Robert A Heinlein

"The trouble with having an open mind, of course, is that people will insist on coming along and trying to put things in it." – Terry Pratchett

"Be careful about reading health books. Some fine day you'll die of a misprint." – Markus Herz

"Two things are infinite: the universe and human stupidity; and I'm not sure about the universe." – Albert Einstein

It wasn't very long before others started bringing things in to share, people stopped snapping at each other, and the holidays went smoother for us.

Another example from my own life was a thing we did with our children now and again. About end of November, we'd look around the neighborhood for those who seemed to be having struggles; one year it was a single mom with three kids who'd been fired from a good job and was working two part time jobs to try and make ends meet. Ours kids knew the kids from school and they'd gone from being pretty average normal kids to being withdrawn; kept to themselves at lunch, carried a lunch that only had peanut butter sandwiches in it. One time my boy came home and said all they'd brought for lunch were three apples. A week before Christmas, I canvassed a few friends for gift cards; my kids and I went out shopping for some things for each child, and Dan took up a collection among his friends-and a week before Christmas, we went to their house with one large box of wrapped gifts, one large box of groceries, a Christmas card that had gift cards from local stores and restaurants, and the left over money from buying the food-which we left on their front porch. We came under cover of darkness, put the stuff on the step, knocked on the door hard, and hid across the street until we were sure the gifts had gone inside. Our kids reported back that the kids came to the last day of school before Christmas break all excited about the surprise from last night.

Every year, we'd bake cookies, enough for ourselves, enough for all the older folks in the church and the Sabbath of Christmas week, we'd hand them out to the seniors. We'd take plates of them to the shut ins as well and deliver them that day. Since the kids had a hand in the making and packaging and gifting, they learned compassion.

I'm sure you can think of someone who needs a lift. Even if you just buy an extra box of Christmas cards, take them to the office, sign them as secret Santa or just "a caring friend"; then hand them out to different people in the office-it will brighten spirits, you'll feel good, and so will others. And you will spread the true meaning of Christmas to those around you. If we all do this, random acts of kindness, what a difference it will make!

But when the fullness of the time had come, God sent forth His Son, born of a woman, born under the law, to redeem those who were under the law, that we might receive the adoption as sons. Galatians 4:4-5

# Day Twenty-Four
# The Music of Christmas

Christmas carols are such a big part of our celebration of
Christmas, from the Messiah which is one long carol of love
from and to God, to the simplest song like Away in a Manger.
The actual list of carols available to sing is huge. The question
you have to ask is, I suppose, just how did we get so many?

If you are a music historian you know that the first carols began
in Europe thousands of years ago. If you want to be strict about
it, they weren't really Christmas carols at all, but pagan songs
sung at the Winter Solstice as people celebrating the return of
the sun danced around stone alters built in circular form. (Think
Stonehenge, for instance.) Winter Solstice happens around
December 22, the shortest day of the year, and the dances were
to ensure that the sun returned the next day and got stronger; the
harder you danced, the stronger the sun would be until we
finally had spring. The word carol actually means dance or a
song of praise and joy! There used to be praise songs written for
all the different seasons, but we seem to have only kept on to
the tradition of Christmas carols. I suppose some of our praise
hymns sung at Easter could be considered as carols.

At any rate, when people converted to Christianity, they brought
the old tunes and songs right along with them; with a little
rewrite, sun became Son, for instance. Way back in 129 A.D., a
Roman Bishop said that a song called "Angel's Hymn" should
be sung at a Christmas service in Rome. We don't have that one
preserved. *Corde natus ex Parentis* (*Of the Father's heart
begotten*) by the Spanish poet Prudentius (d. 413) is still around

and is sung-I recall doing it in choir as a teen. Jesus Refulsit Omnium" "Jesus, Light of All the Nations" written by St. Hilary of Poitiers, the 4th century mystic, is still used in come communions. It has an eerie, ethereal sound to it.

The difficulty was that these early hymns were all in Latin, didn't have the rousing fun of the pagan carols and simply weren't that accessible or singable for the average person. People stopped celebrating Christmas almost altogether except for exchanging presents with each other and having parties. All that changed with St. Francis of Assisi in 1223 when he started his Nativity Plays in Italy. The people in the plays sang songs or 'canticles' that told the story during the plays. Some were in Latin but more and more they were in the language of the people and were very singable. People could understand them and join right in. The new carols spread to France, Spain, Germany and other European countries.

Most Carols from this time and the Elizabethan period are fables, loosely based on the Christmas story, (I mean, most of them have a baby n a manger there somewhere, but talking donkeys, sudden flowers booming in the snow, that sort of thing were quite popular.) They were not really considered religious songs; the differentiation of secular from sacred blurred quite a lot. Traveling singers called minstrels sang these carols; the words were changed for the local people wherever they were traveling. One carol that is still with us from this era is 'I Saw Three Ships'. It was finally settled down and printed in a final form in 1833.

When the Puritans came to power in England in 1640s, the celebration of Christmas and singing carols was stopped by the government. It was seen as too frivolous, a waste of time and money and anti-sacred if not downright pagan. However, the carols survived as people sang them in secret and celebrated in secret as well, much more subdued than before, but still occurring. Carols stayed mainly unsung until Victorian times, when two men called William Sandys and Davis Gilbert collected lots of old music from villagers in England. Their work spread rapidly all over. It started first, as always, with the professional singers, called "waits"; bands of people led by local leaders who had the legal right to take money in public from folks. (Taking money in public seemed like begging and that was illegal too.) They only sang on Christmas Eve (called watchnight). They were supposedly singing as the shepherds had eons ago as they waiting for the Christ to be born. They collected alms as they sang.

At the same time, orchestras and choirs set up in the cities for public performance, and people wanted to sing what they were hearing, so carols again became popular. Good King Wenceslas was written during the Victorian era.

Shortly, caroling in the streets, as seen in Dickens Christmas Carol, got very popular. Christmas eve services in churches became a tradition, Candlelight services being quite the thing. We still have these today.

After popular music and musicians began writing in earnest for Christmas in the late 1800's, Hollywood and Nashville took over, so we ended up with everyone from Bing Crosby to John Denver putting out Christmas albums. Everyone loves

Christmas music in some genre, from the secular (Grandma got Ran Over by a Reindeer) to the melancholy (I'll Be Home for Christmas, popular in WWII) to the divine (Messiah). They speak to our hearts; they lift our souls and they make the season bright.

"Let us have music for Christmas…
Sound the trumpet of joy and rebirth;
Let each of us try, with a song in our hearts,
To bring peace to men on earth."
~ Mildred L. Jarrell

# Day Twenty-Five

## A Pickle? Really?

Why did I end our readings with the fable of the pickle? Isn't that sort of odd?

No, it's come full circle; from the nativity to the commercial. You have no doubt seen pickle ornaments to hang in your tree and wondered why, just as with the spider webs, people put those in a Christmas tree. Most folks see pickles as something on a relish plate, not made out of glass and shiny. Here is how the pickle started.

Back in the late1880's the era of five and dime stores (which led up to department stores, big box stores, etc.), the gentleman who owned and operated Woolworth's Five and Dime store started selling glass ornaments imported cheaply from Germany. People loved them and fragile as they were, kept buying them to replace what got broken. (Just like today, I suspect the family cat was just as entranced by the shiny thing and knocked them off; as did toddlers.) Some of the original boxes of ornaments included glass nativity scenes, winter sleds and trees and one collection had fruits and vegetable-including a pickle. When asked why, Woolworth's claimed it was an old tradition in Germany that whoever found the pickle in the tree got to have the first gift. It was always the last ornament hung on the tree, when the children were not present, and hence, the first child who found it got the first gift. The only problem was, no one in Germany had any idea what they were talking about! It seems to have been the invention of a very inventive ad person. However, the idea caught on and many folks today have a pickle on their tree.

Now there are two other stories concerning pickles on Christmas trees, that I really like better, but are most likely not as accurate as the above story, but I wanted to share them.

There was a young soldier in the Civil War who was born in Bavaria (That's in Germany now). He was a prisoner of war; he was starving and he begged a guard for just the pickle off his sandwich before he died. The guard took pity on the dying young soldier and gave him the pickle slice because it was Christmas eve. The pickle gave the young man enough strength to hang on one more day, and the next day the jail was attacked by the Northern soldiers, liberated and he lived! So every year thereafter, he put a pickle on his Christmas tree as a remembrance. His first was supposedly a hand carved wooden one.

St. Nicholas is involved in the other tale, and it's one of the more macabre. It's a medieval tale of two young boys traveling home from a boarding school to spend the holiday with their family. They stopped at an inn for the night to sleep, and the innkeeper, seeing they had money in their pouches for the trip, waited until they were asleep, murdered them, took their money and stuffed their bodies in an old pickle barrel until he could take them out and bury them. St. Nicholas stopped at the same inn, was directed by an angel to open the barrel, found the bodies in the barrel and miraculously bought them back to life! The angel of death took the evil innkeeper instead of the boys and St. Nicholas took the boys safely to their homes.

My best guess is that a Christmas ornament salesman had too much inventory and invented all three stories to download his inventory...after all, up until the legends started, how popular would a pickle ornament have been? Well, just in case you were wondering...

The little town of Berrien Springs, MI was known as the Christmas Pickle Capital of the World from 1992 until 2003. They now call the festival, "Kindle Your Christmas Spirit." They grow a lot of cucumbers there and they had a parade and festivities. Folks who lived there in that era remember fondly the parade led by the Grand Dillmeister, who passed out fresh pickles along the parade route. You could purchase Christmas Pickle Ornament from the Museum Store, or a pair of gurken earrings or Chocolate-Covered Sweet Pickles. It didn't attract enough tourists so they switched it to what was considered a little more marketable. That's too bad.

 We tell all those stories to lead up to what is the actual story of Christmas, the most familiar being Luke 2:1-20.

"And it came to pass in those days *that* a decree went out from Caesar Augustus that all the world should be registered. This census first took place while Quirinius was governing Syria. So all went to be registered, everyone to his own city. Joseph also went up from Galilee, out of the city of Nazareth, into Judea, to the city of David, which is called Bethlehem, because he was of the house and lineage of David, to be registered with Mary, his betrothed wife, who was with child. So it was, that while they were there, the days were completed for her to be delivered. And she brought forth her firstborn Son, and wrapped

107

Him in swaddling clothes, and laid Him in a manger, because there was no room for them in the inn

Now there were in the same country shepherds living out in the fields, keeping watch over their flock by night. And behold, an angel of the Lord stood before them, and the glory of the Lord shone around them, and they were greatly afraid. Then the angel said to them, "Do not be afraid, for behold, I bring you good tidings of great joy which will be to all people.  For there is born to you this day in the city of David a Savior, who is Christ the Lord. And this *will be* the sign to you: You will find a Babe wrapped in swaddling clothes, lying in a manger."

And suddenly there was with the angel a multitude of the heavenly host praising God and saying:

"Glory to God in the highest,
And on earth peace, goodwill toward men!"

So it was, when the angels had gone away from them into heaven, that the shepherds said to one another, "Let us now go to Bethlehem and see this thing that has come to pass, which the Lord has made known to us."  And they came with haste and found Mary and Joseph, and the Babe lying in a manger. Now when they had seen *Him,* they made widely known the saying which was told them concerning this Child. And all those who heard *it* marveled at those things which were told them by the shepherds. But Mary kept all these things and pondered *them* in her heart. Then the shepherds returned, glorifying and praising God for all the things that they had heard and seen, as it was told them."

The wise men don't show up until later. So how could such a simple tale written by a physician hold such power; how could what have happened have lasted so long, been adopted by so many in so many countries, and given rise to so many tales about what was really a birth of a baby? What was so different here?

I'm not a theologian, but from what I have read and heard, for centuries before He came, there were prophecies written down about His birth- I am told they span from Genesis to Malachi, and there are 55 of them. His arrival must have been important to God to have told prophets fifty-five times it was going to happen, and to give exact facts about it-things like there would be a star, a special star, the child would be Jewish, of the lineage of King David, born of a virgin, in Bethlehem, there would be Kings presenting him gifts (the Magi), that Herod would overreact and kill the babies in Bethlehem-that's just a few of the many predictions, all fifty-five of which came true.

If I were to speak to you personally, I suspect you'd have some tales from your life of things and events around Christmas, I've shared a few with you along the way. Somehow, two thousand years later, we still think of this one child, this one life and all it has meant to us; how the season has impacted us as we grew, some of us in poverty so it was more a strain than a blessing, some have fond memories of family get togethers, some not. All have been impacted in some way by the birth of this one person and this one time in history. From just Mary, Joseph and the shepherds to the Christian faith around the globe, at last count 2.18 billion alive today, to all the billions who have believed and died since that time. One life impacted so many for so long; you could say His birth changed the world. What would have happened had He not come?

As you celebrate this year, by yourself, with a family, however it comes to be for you, may the Lord above bless you in this blessed Advent and Christmas season.

# Additional Fun things you might want to try this season

(my idea of an appendix)

# Recipes to make, share and enjoy

Here are just a few cookie recipes we've used in our family through the years: try some, share some, and let the fragrance of baking something from scratch increase your enjoyment and peace.

One of my son Tristain's favorites:

1 box of mint Oreo cookies, crushed to smithereens

1 bar of cream cheese, softened

Mix the Oreos and the cream cheese until well blended-use a food processor, it's simpler and you avoid someone sneaking off with some of the Oreos before you're done.

Form the mix into 1.5 inch balls and set on parchment on a cookie sheet. Put in the freezer to get cold for thirty minutes.

Melt white chocolate (almond bark works well) in a double boiler slowly.

Take the Oreo balls, dip them in the melted chocolate, and set back on the parchment paper to harden. You can drizzle melted semi-sweet chocolate chips on them as decoration or dip them in edible glitter before you set them down to dry. They must be refrigerated if they make it that long-around our house they last about one meal.

**Christmas Gingerbread Sandwishes** (Ben couldn't say sandwich when he was three, so the name stuck)

2 1/2 c. all-purpose flour

2 1/2 tsp. ground ginger

1 1/2 tsp. Cinnamon

1/2 tsp. ground nutmeg

1/2 tsp. baking soda

1/4 tsp. ground cloves

1/4 tsp. kosher salt

1/2 c. (1 stick) unsalted butter, at room temp.

1/2 c. firmly packed dark brown sugar

1 large egg

1/4 c. molasses

1 1/2 tsp. pure vanilla extract

Sanding sugar and white pearl dragees, for decorating

**For the frosting**

1/2 c. (1 stick) unsalted butter, at room temp

1/3 c. confectioners' sugar

Salt - just a pinch, no more

4 oz. milk chocolate, melted and cooled to room temp

**Directions**

1. In a large bowl, whisk together the flour, ginger, cinnamon, nutmeg, baking soda, cloves and salt.

2. Using an electric mixer, beat the butter and brown sugar in a large bowl until light and fluffy, about 3 minutes. Beat in the egg, molasses and vanilla. Reduce the mixer speed to low and gradually add the flour mixture, mixing until just incorporated (the dough will be soft).

3. Divide the dough in portions and roll each between 2 sheets parchment paper to 1/8 in. thick. Refrigerate until firm, at least 30 minutes or wrap and refrigerate for up to 1 week.

4. Heat oven to 350°F. Line baking sheets with parchment paper. Using floured 3-inch hexagon or round cookie cutters, cut out cookies. Place on prepared sheets. Reroll, chill and cut scraps.

5. Bake, rotating positions of baking sheets halfway through, until cookies are light golden brown around edges, 10 to 12 min. Let cool on sheets for 5 minutes before transferring to wire racks to cool completely.

6. Meanwhile, make chocolate frosting: Using an electric mixer, beat butter, sugar, and pinch salt on medium until light and fluffy. Reduce speed to low and add melted chocolate, beating to combine.

7. Decorate half of the ginger cookies with sanding sugar, and dragees, as desired. Spread chocolate frosting on remaining cookie halves and sandwich with decorated halves.

# Yum's

So easy!

Ingredients

2 cups of graham cookie crumbs

2 sticks of butter

1 pkg (8 oz)semisweet chocolate chips

1 pkg (8 oz) butterscotch chips

1 pkg sweetened shredded coconut

2 can's condensed milk

mix melted butter with the cracker crumbs: press into a 9 x 12 pan

sprinkle the coconut smoothly over this

add the chocolate chips over the coconut in another smooth layer

spread the condensed milk over top

Bake at 3?50 until lightly browned and everything has melted together in a lovely mush of sweetness.

Allow to cool completely, cut into bars.

Keep in a tight plastic box or tin until you want to eat them or until the kids find them or worst yet, your husband, who will walk off with them to the den and you won't see the cookies or the container for months…

**Honeybees**

Another unbaked recipe you can have your kids help make

1 cup peanut putter

1 cup dry milk

½ cup maple syrup or honey

sliced almonds

cocoa powder-just a small amount

confectionery sugar-again, small amount

Smoosh peanut butter, milk and honey together until smooth.
Form into tiny little ovals, about 1.5 inches long.
Push two slices of almond on each side for wings. Take a
toothpick, dampen it, stick it into the cocoa and lay it across the
back of the cookie for stripes. Store all in fridge.

OR

if the kids are too big or you don't have time, instead of
individual bees, from the dough into a roll, sprinkle
confectionery sugar and chopped nuts or cocoa powder on a
piece of wax paper, roll the dough in it until you have a short
tube, then roll the wax paper around it and put it in the fridge
until cold, then slice it to serve. Or break off pieces and nibble.

Dan's favorite Cookies
**Date nut bars**
3 cups chopped dates
1/1/2 cups water
¼ or less sugar
Put the above in a sauce pan, cook slowly until it is a smooth, spreadable filling
Meantime in a bowl combined:
1 cup brown sugar-again1 cup melted butter
When smooth, add 1 ¾ cup flour
1 ½ cup quick oats
¼ cup pecan flour
½ tsp baking powder-j1/2 tsp salt


Once mixed, press half in the bottom of a 9 x 12 pan, pour the date mixture over that, and sprinkle the rest of the oat mixture over the dates. Pat them all together, then put in a 350 oven for 25 minutes. You have to cut them with a warm blade into 36 bars. Really don't wait or they get all crumbly on you. Let them cool after taking out of the pan and cooling on a cooling rack.

## Thumbprint cookies

1/4 cup butter softened
1/4 cup shortening
1/4 cup firmly packed brown sugar
1 egg divided
1 teaspoon vanilla
1 cup flour all purpose
pinch salt
1 cup walnuts finely chopped
raspberry jam seedless preferred or any other jam you like, or
soft buttercreme frosting in nice colors

Preheat oven to 350°F. (Honestly if it is cookie baking day, the oven is already on because you know you can't just try one recipe)
Cream butter, shortening and brown sugar until fluffy. Add egg yolk and vanilla. (Set egg white aside in a small bowl.) Combine flour and salt and add in a little at a time until blended well.
Divide dough into 20 pieces and roll into balls. Beat egg white in a small bowl. Dip each cookie dough ball in the egg whites and then roll into the nuts, pressing to stick them well.
Place each ball of dough about 2″ apart and using the end of a spoon or your thumb, make an indentation in each cookie. Seal any cracks that form on the sides. Freeze 15-20 minutes.
Bake 16-18 minutes or until set. Remove from the oven and use the back of a 1/2 teaspoon to press the indents again if needed.
Fill indents with jam or icing. Cool completely.

## Kissing cookies

Worth getting a kiss for baking…

Ingredients
  1/2 cup light brown sugar packed
  1/2 cup granulated sugar
  1/2 cup unsalted butter softened
  1/2 cup creamy peanut butter
  1 large egg at room temperature
  1 teaspoon vanilla extract
  1 3/4 cup all-purpose flour
  1 teaspoon baking soda
  1/4 teaspoon kosher salt
  1/2 cup granulated sugar (for rolling the dough in)
Hershey's kisses, unwrapped (One year Ben was helping and he didn't unwrap them…makes a mess. Do not try…)

1.  Blend together in a bowl brown sugar, 1/2 cup granulated sugar, softened butter and peanut butter. Using a hand mixer (or stand mixer if you have one), beat on medium speed until light and fluffy, about 1-2 minutes.
2.  Add egg and vanilla and beat until well mixed. Add flour, baking soda, and salt, and beat on LOW until combined and no flour streaks remain. Scrape the bowl as needed.
3.  Cover bowl with plastic wrap and refrigerate for 30 minutes or more. (You know you can mix all these and have them sitting in your fridge the night before and then take them out one at a time, assemble and bake them?) Add unwrapped chocolate kisses to a bowl and refrigerate as well, until ready to add to baked cookies.
4.  When ready to bake, preheat oven to 375 F degrees. Line a baking sheet with a sheet of parchment paper and set aside. Add final 1/2 cup granulated sugar to a small shallow bowl, and set aside.

5. Shape dough into balls a little larger than 1 inch in diameter. Gently roll balls in bowl of granulated sugar to coat on all sides.
6. Place approximately 2 inches apart on prepared baking sheet and bake 9-10 minutes, until lightly golden brown and tops of cookies have a cracked appearance.
7. Press a chocolate kiss into the center of each cookie, mashing it down a little, and they will melt together a little. Remove to a cooling rack to continue cooling.

OK, another of my husband Dan's favorites-really, I think he just likes coconut. And mint. And chocolate. And any combination of the same…

Coconut Macaroons

## Ingredients
- 1 14- ounce bag sweetened flaked coconut
- 1 14- ounce can sweetened condensed milk
- 2 cups chocolate chips divided use (can use semisweet or milk chocolate)
- 1/2 cup chopped almonds plus 30 whole almonds for garnish

1. Preheat the oven to 350°F. Line a sheet pan with parchment paper or a non-stick baking mat.
2. In a large bowl, mix together the coconut, condensed milk, 1 cup of chocolate chips and 1/2 cup chopped almonds. Stir until thoroughly combined.
3. Drop 2 tablespoons of the dough onto the sheet pan approximately 1 1/2 inches apart. Wet your fingers and firmly pat the dough into cookie shapes; just sort of flatten them and tuck them around a little to be 3/8 inch thick and sort of round.
4. Bake for 10-12 minutes, or until edges are lightly browned. Repeat the process with the remaining dough.
5. Place 1 cup of chocolate chips in a microwave safe bowl. Microwave in 30 second increments until chocolate is melted. Stir until smooth.
6. Drizzle approximately 1 teaspoon of melted chocolate over the top of each cookie. Place an almond into the center of each cookie on top of the melted chocolate.
7. Let the chocolate harden then serve, or store in an airtight container at room temperature for up to 5 day or until my son Miah and his boys gets here at which time all bets are

off as to how long they last. Those grandkids are turning into cookie monsters, but they have a great mentor.

**Mint bars-**not as hard as they look and ever so tasty…

**Ingredients**
**BOTTOM LAYER**
- 1 cup chocolate chips
- 1/2 cup butter
- 1 1/4 cup graham crumbs
- 1 cup flaked coconut
- 1/2 cup chopped pecans

**MINT LAYER**
- 2 cups powdered sugar
- 1/4 cup butter
- 3 tablespoons milk
- 2 tablespoons cornstarch
- ½ tsp vanilla
- 1 teaspoon mint extract or crème de menthe, if you can find it
- green food coloring

**TOP LAYER**
- 3/4 cup chocolate chips
- 2 teaspoons oil

**Instructions**
1. Line a 9×9 pan with parchment paper.
2. Melt the butter & chocolate chips for the bottom layer in a small bowl.
3. Add graham crumbs, coconut and chopped pecans. Mix well and press into the bottom of the pan. Refrigerate until completely cooled.
4. Beat all ingredients for the mint layer on medium until completely combined. Spread over the cooled base. Refrigerate.
5. Microwave oil and chocolate chips on medium heat until just melted. Spread over mint layer. Cool completely and cut into squares.

I always make a double batch and use a 9 x 12 pan because the smaller version won't make it long enough to speak about.

**Words to favorite Carols, so you can hum along and sing while baking:**

The Friendly Beasts (12th century)

1.Jesus our brother, kind and good
Was humbly born in a stable rude
And the friendly beasts around Him stood,
Jesus our brother, kind and good.

2. "I," said the donkey, shaggy and brown,
"I carried His mother up hill and down;
I carried her safely to Bethlehem town."
"I," said the donkey, shaggy and brown.

3. "I," said the cow all white and red
"I gave Him my manger for His bed;
I gave him my hay to pillow his head."
"I," said the cow all white and red.

4. "I," said the sheep with curly horn,
"I gave Him my wool for His blanket warm;
He wore my coat on Christmas morn."
"I," said the sheep with curly horn.

5. "I," said the dove from the rafters high,
"I cooed Him to sleep so He would not cry;
We cooed him to sleep, my mate and I."
"I," said the dove from the rafters high.

6. Thus every beast by some good spell,
In the stable dark was glad to tell
Of the gift he gave Immanuel,
The gift he gave Immanuel.

Angels we have heard on high,
Singing sweetly through the night,
And the mountains in reply
Echoing their brave delight.
Gloria in excelsis Deo.
Gloria in excelsis Deo.

Shepherds, why this jubilee?
Why these songs of happy cheer?
What great brightness did you see?
What glad tiding did you hear?
Gloria in excelsis Deo.
Gloria in excelsis Deo.

Come to Bethlehem and see
Him whose birth the angels sing;
Come, adore on bended knee
Christ, the Lord, the new-born King.
Gloria in excelsis Deo.
Gloria in excelsis Deo.

See him in a manger laid
Whom the angels praise above;
Mary, Joseph, lend your aid,
While we raise our hearts in love.
Gloria in excelsis Deo.
Gloria in excelsis Deo.

What Child is this, who laid to rest,
On Mary's lap is sleeping?
Whom angels greet with anthems sweet
While shepherds watch are keeping?
This, this is Christ the King
Whom shepherds guard and angels sing.
Haste, haste to bring Him laud,
The Babe, the Son of Mary.

Why lies He in such mean estate
Where ox and ass are feeding?
Good Christian, fear: for sinners here,
The silent Word is pleading.
This, this is Christ the King
Whom shepherds guard and angels sing.
Haste, haste to bring Him laud,
The Babe, the Son of Mary.

Nails, spear, shall pierce Him through,
The Cross be borne, for me, for you:
Hail, hail, the Word made flesh,
The Babe, the Son of Mary!
This, this is Christ the King
Whom shepherds guard and angels sing.
Haste, haste to bring Him laud,
The Babe, the Son of Mary.

So bring Him incense, gold and myrrh;
Come peasant, king to own Him.
The King of Kings salvation brings;
Let loving hearts enthrone Him.
This, this is Christ the King
Whom shepherds guard and angels sing.
Haste, haste to bring Him laud,
The Babe, the Son of Mary.

Raise, raise, the song on high,
The Virgin sings her lullaby:
Joy, joy for Christ is born,
The Babe, the Son of Mary!
This, this is Christ the King
Whom shepherds guard and angels sing.
Haste, haste to bring Him laud,
The Babe, the Son of Mary.

Bring A Torch, Jeanette Isabella

French carol, ca. 1553

Bring a torch, Jeanette, Isabella
Bring a torch, come swiftly and run
Christ is born,
tell the folk of the village
Jesus is sleeping in His cradle
Ah, ah, beautiful is the Mother
Ah, ah, beautiful is her Son
Hasten now, good folk of the village
Hasten now, the Christ Child to see
You will find Him asleep in the manger
Quietly come and whisper softly
Hush, hush, peacefully now He slumbers
Hush, hush, peacefully now He sleeps


**Away in a Manger**

Away in a manger, no crib for his bed,
the little Lord Jesus laid down his sweet head.
The stars in the bright sky looked down where he lay,
The little Lord Jesus asleep on the hay.

The cattle are lowing, the baby awakes,
but little Lord Jesus no crying he makes.
I love thee, Lord Jesus! Look down from the sky,
And stay by my side until morning is nigh.

Good Christian Men, Rejoice

John Mason Neale, 19th century

Good Christian men, rejoice
With heart and soul and voice;
Give ye heed to what we say:
  News! News!
  Jesus Christ is born today:
Ox and ass before him bow
And He is in the manger now.
  Christ is born today!
  Christ is born today!

Good Christian men, rejoice
With heart and soul and voice;
Now ye hear of endless bliss;
  Joy! Joy!
  Jesus Christ was born for this!
He has oped the heav'nly door
And man is blessed evermore.
  Christ was born for this!
  Christ was born for this!

Good Christian men, rejoice
With heart and soul and voice;
Now ye need not fear the grave;
  Peace! Peace!
  Jesus Christ was born to save!
Calls you one and calls you all
To gain his everlasting hall.
  Christ was born to save!
  Christ was born to save!

Coventry Carol

Lully, lullay, thou little tiny child,
Bye bye, lully, lullay.
Lully, lullay, thou little tiny child,
Bye bye, lully, lullay.

O sisters too, how may we do
For to preserve this day
This poor youngling for whom we sing,
"Bye bye, lully, lullay"?

Herod the king, in his raging,
Charged he hath this day
His men of might in his own sight
All young children to slay.

That woe is me, poor child, for thee
And ever mourn and may
For thy parting neither say nor sing,
"Bye bye, lully, lullay."

## Carol of the Bells

Hark! how the bells
Sweet silver bells
All seem to say,
"Throw cares away."
Christmas is here
Bringing good cheer
To young and old
Meek and the bold

Ding, dong, ding, dong
That is their song
With joyful ring
All caroling
One seems to hear
Words of good cheer
From everywhere
Filling the air

Oh how they pound,
Raising the sound,
O'er hill and dale,
Telling their tale,
Gaily they ring
While people sing
Songs of good cheer
Christmas is here
Merry, merry, merry, merry Christmas
Merry, merry, merry, merry Christmas

On, on they send
On without end

Their joyful tone
To every home

Ding, dong, ding, dong.

J. Traveler Pelton was born in West Virginia in the last century. She is wife to Dan (45 years!), mother of six adults, a grandmother of eight, a Clinically Licensed Independent Social Worker with Supervisory Status, at present in private practice, a retired adjunct professor of social work at her local university and an insatiable reader. She is a cancer survivor. Traveler avidly studies science and technology, fascinated by the inventiveness of people. She is quick to draw parallels in different fields and weave stories around them. Traveler is a fabric artist and her most enjoyable time is spent spinning yarn while spinning yarns for the grandkids…

You can reach Traveler at her website:

travelerpelton.com

Or like us and share us on Facebook at Traveler Pelton

Or write to us by snail mail at

Springhaven Croft

216 Sychar Rd.

Mt. Vernon, OH 43050

<u>She loves to hear from her readers!</u>

All our books are available on Amazon as both eBook and print copy, Kindle unlimited as free downloads

# <u>We'd love it if you'd leave us a review!</u>

**Your Attention Please!!!!**

<u>Would you like to join the team at Potpourri Books?</u>

Traveler is <u>always</u> looking for responsible beta readers for her new books. A beta reader gets a prepublication copy of all new books, <u>free of charge</u> in exchange for an honest review written on Amazon, and a short email letting her know of any glitches you may have found that got past the editor, any suggestions you may have, and your opinion of the book. What else do you get out of it?

A beta reader gets:

A free download of one of her already published books and

as soon as your review of that book gets placed on Amazon,

free downloads of her already published works: for each review, you get a free book.

And

A free copy pre publication copy of all new books…

And

Other neat freebies as they come, from bookmarks to stickers to posters to pens to neat things I find to send out to my betas-

Interested?

Contact Traveler at

travelerpelton@gmail.com for more info…

*We would love to add you to the team!*

Thank you for enjoying this little book about my favorite season of the year. If you enjoyed it, perhaps you would enjoy my book Ninety Days to the God Habit. It's all about finding the presence of God in your life on a daily basis. It makes a wonderful gift for yourself or your loved ones. Here's an excerpt:

## Introduction

Curiosity and the Spirit made you pick up this book: the idea of escaping a hum-drum, inadequate form of spirituality has intrigued that part of you that still has hope; the normality of having a commonplace experience instead of what God intended gnaws at the edge of your mind. If you are reading this book, I am assuming the idea of getting closer to God in just a few short weeks has intrigued you, whetted your appetite and touched your soul. You may be a searcher, or someone dissatisfied with a lukewarm state of soul or you may be someone who has long walked with Him and feel that for some reason nothing is working anymore. You feel as if the prayer warrior within you has gone on vacation and shows no sign of coming back from the beach.

At any rate, you have tried and failed to set up anything that has worked for long to bring you closer to God and the peace of mind that brings. You are tired of halfway change. Your Christianity has turned into yearly resolutions that are kept about as well as sudden diets. You may think the routine of daily life does not allow you time to bring yourself in sync with God; there are not enough hours in the day to pray and study; keep up with everything leaves you feeling dissatisfied and upset. Whatever the reason, you are looking for some way, some reason, some formula or schematic or equation to make the unease go away. I felt that way once and what I learned about escaping that feeling is the rationale behind this book. I have hope for you, based on my own experience, solid provable research into how your mind works and a faith that this is what God wants me to write for you. I was where you are once. I found a way out, and I want you to come along the constantly narrowing path to God-achievers.

Among the roles I fill in my life are Wife, Mother, Grandmother, church planter, shepherd, farmer, author, artist and Social Worker. The ways people live their lives fascinates me. I never have quite enough time to read all the journal studies done about people. I do try, although sometimes I find it's hard to comb through all the jargon to find small nuggets of truth that I find useful in my work in counseling and coaching people. Over the years, the gleaning and application of what I learn while doing private study to what people who come to me need is a cause and effect sort of serendipity not unlike a choir or music group playing; you know it works, but unless you're the orchestra conductor or the composer you are never quite sure how it goes together, it simply does and it makes the listening a pleasure. The aha! moments I see in my office as something clicks within people is a wonder I don't get over. I like to see it happen so I keep track of what seems to be the most problematic for my patients and for my church members and then I go into research mode to find answers for them and in doing so, often find it helps me as well. In the last few years of work, I have noticed people are frustrated by mediocrity; they are tired of the sameness, they want something to pull them to a safer shore, but a shore where there is creativity and kindness, love and no loneliness, a place of acceptance and energy. They want to make changes, especially within their spiritual lives, but the habit of get up, eat, work, home again, shower, TV/social media and sleep, over and over, is killing them. The habits of a drone like existence makes them lonely, angry, bitter and helpless. Since we weren't designed to be hermits, nor to run along a hamster trail, it's no wonder our habits are destroying our lives.

A short while back, I got very interested in habits; habits being automatic behaviors that have been wired into our brains through repetition; I wanted to find out what it takes to make them, what it takes to break them, how we can control them. Too many of the people I work with were struggling with stopping the consequences of habits they'd made early in life and now were paying for, yet felt helpless to do anything. Their habits were killing them. They'd developed them early in life and they wanted them to go away. They wouldn't go easily without a struggle and the struggle is what we need to make stop. You can't get rid of consequences; they happen as cause and effect. For instance, you smoke two packs a day for twenty years, you will most likely develop lung cancer or some form of lung disease. Will stopping smoking stop the disease? No, of course not. It will help you get stronger, but you will still have to fight the cancer battle which your own actions caused to occur.

It's a little like taming lions. When a lion is little, (or so I am told. I do not raise lions, only children, alpaca, Pomeranians, canaries and Siamese cats) when a lion is less than three months old, they are cuddly and easy to play with and they are simple to get away from. You stand up, slip them off your lap and walk away. They may give chase but they really aren't all that hurtful. When a lion grows larger, say nine months, they are much more determined, stronger, and it might take someone helping you, interceding as it were, to get away from a determined young lion. You'll come away with bites, scratches and a decided decision not to go in that cage again. But once a lion is full grown, you need someone with a gun or a tranquilizer dart to slow it down or kill it outright and you will not get out unscathed. You will get hurt. You could even die. The same is true for habits. You can smoke a cigarette or a joint once or twice with friends and put it down. You can overindulge on alcohol, or tell white lies, or cheat on your taxes and probably get away with it for a time. You can neglect to pray daily, and think to come back to it. As time goes on, and you continue to smoke, the poisons that are addictive get stronger and harder to overcome. You can still stop doing it, but you may need some help, like nicotine patches, a support group or a good scare from your doctor. As time goes on, not praying, not actively putting God first will gradually lead to a sort of spiritual ennui that is much like Alzheimer's-you remember things in the past but the present state of your soul eludes you. The Spirit wants to talk to you, and sometimes you rouse yourself enough to go to a revival meeting for a few days, but after the hype is over, you slip and nothing changes except the load of guilt you feel.

If you have neglected God for some time, you are going to need to put some effort into getting back into His throne room, feeling comfortable with His presence again. Do not think I am saying He has left you; no, but just as any other earthly friend, you can drift apart and the first steps back into friendship feel awkward; after asking about the job, and the kids and the weather, what do you talk about? You can restart your spiritual life, you can regain the place you once held in His presence and feel His help, but you may need some prodding from someone who loves you. He knew that and He sent us his Holy Spirit to get us to remember just when we need it. (John 14:26 But the Helper, the Holy Spirit, whom the Father will send in My name, He will teach you all things, and bring to your remembrance all things that I said to you.)

I know from experience, the longer you let it wait, put it aside, and think I'll do it tonight, or tomorrow morning, or when Lent comes or it's going to be my New Years' resolution next year, you come to the place where it seems too hard, there are simply too many distractions to read the Bible, or think of Him, or talk to Him. You have officially drifted and eventually that Old Serpent will whisper you've gone too far, it's too hard, you're too busy, nobody does that anymore and you wander into a complacent mode. You know you're a Christian although you can't quite remember to call on Him when needed, or where that verse in the Bible was that you need right now, and your soul somewhat closes its' spiritual eyes and goes to sleep. The Spirit, in an attempt to wake you up, sometimes resorts to extreme measures to get your attention, and sometimes, even that doesn't work anymore. Has God moved? No, you lost anchor, you are out to sea and you need rescued. When it gets that far, you need a complete revival, a re-doing of your habits, a turning back, repentance if you will, in order to regain that first love, that flush of affection, that security that He is there for you. It's

153

not something to day dream about or reminisce about, it's a call to action. Sometimes something out of the ordinary comes along and you suddenly realize you've neglected Him so much you're afraid to talk to Him. The cancer comes or the car wreck happens, or the marriage problems start, you lose your job, whatever the crisis may be, and you find yourself lost with no one to comfort you and you wonder where is God? He didn't go anywhere. You wandered. The fact that you have gotten a copy of this book may be a leading of the Spirit to bring you back to Him. This book is written to help you find your straight path out of the bad habit of ignoring the Lord of the Universe and engaging in behavior that will being you closer to heaven. This book will help you develop a habit of putting God first and accepting His leading and His rewards.

So if you're trying to get back to Him, or perhaps you never knew Him in the first place, or perhaps you're a new believer and wanted to make changes in the right way, whichever is the case, let me assure you, He is a gentleman, He is a lover, He is still there waiting for you to make an appointment with Him every day. The question you ask me is simple: how do I get from point A-which is where I am- to point B, where I want to be, in the shortest, fastest way possible? I am glad you asked. With a prayer and a song, let's begin our odyssey, the pilgrimage we are beginning to activate our God Habit.

# Day Eighty-nine

**Romans 8:6**

**"For to be carnally minded is death, but to be spiritually minded is life and peace".**

"Church people" have a real problem.

You've probably seen it. We are so good! We don't drink, smoke, do drugs, live fast, dress wrong, use too much makeup or jewelry, we pay tithe, we go to church, we exercise, we sleep right, we do good, we support the right causes – and many of us are probably lost.

You see, living a good, moral life will not save you. You will not make yourself righteous by hard work. Sure, you won't fry your brain, you might live longer, you'll be less prone get cancer, but you'll burn just as long as any other sinner if you don't get right with God.

What consolation will it be to know you behaved yourself if you're lost?

If you live a moral life, you won't go to jail. You'll probably live a long time, and have a respected role in your community. But most likely, you will not be happy.

You see, you will always have an empty spot inside you. There will be a longing, a desire for something intangible. You will run as fast as you can to do and achieve and gain, and will fail just at the end of your journey.

The only thing that will cure the ache within is Christ's righteousness. The only thing that will save you is your relationship with Him. Anything else is just frivolity and time wasting. Being moral will not bring you righteousness, but righteousness from Christ will make you over and make you truly moral. Righteousness is found in a person. And that person is Jesus.

I am trying here to prevent anyone saying the really foolish thing that people often say about Him: "I'm ready to accept Jesus as a great moral teacher, but I don't accept his claim to be God". That is the one thing we must not say. A man who was merely a man and said the sort of things Jesus said would not be a great moral teacher. He would either be a lunatic — on the level with the man who says he is a poached egg — or else he would be the Devil of Hell. You must make your choice. Either this man was, and is, the Son of God, or else a madman or something worse. You can shut him up for a fool, you can spit at him and kill him as a demon or you can fall at his feet and call him Lord and God, but let us not come with any patronizing nonsense about his being a great human teacher. He has not left that open to us. He did not intend to. "

C. S. Lewis

# Day Ninety

*John 12:26*

**If anyone serves Me, let him follow Me; and where I am, there My servant will be also. If anyone serves Me, him My Father will honor.**

What an honor it is to serve God!

By serving him, we accomplish many things: we build our faith, and that of those who we encounter, we build our trust in Him; and we show the world that it is possible to follow God. It is more than figuratively being a light or salt or what have you; it's real.

Remember the story of the Velveteen rabbit?

'Real isn't how you are made,' said the Skin Horse. 'It's a thing that happens to you. When a child loves you for a long, long time, not just to play with, but REALLY loves you, then you become Real.'

'Does it hurt?' asked the Rabbit.

'Sometimes,' said the Skin Horse, for he was always truthful. 'When you are Real you don't mind being hurt.'

'Does it happen all at once, like being wound up,' he asked, 'or bit by bit?'

'It doesn't happen all at once,' said the Skin Horse. 'You

become. It takes a long time. That's why it doesn't happen often to people who break easily, or have sharp edges, or who have to be carefully kept. Generally, by the time you are Real, most of your hair has been loved off, and your eyes drop out and you get loose in the joints and very shabby. But these things don't matter at all, because once you are Real you can't be ugly, except to people who don't understand."

(Margery Williams Bianco, The Velveteen Rabbit)

Sometimes the people of God may look worn, or tired, but they have an inner glow, a joy in life, that grows out of their love for Him and for others.

The story is told of the founder of the Salvation Army. He had just enough means to send a one word telegram to his struggling workers. His chosen word? "Others."

We love God by our work for Others. Not that it saves us, not that it perfects us, but because we are real, and as Real Christians, we cannot help but serve and love and give, just as Christ did before us. It is an honor and a privilege to serve Him.

Salvation is the free gift of God; it results in service to Him and to His others.

"You will find all of theology summed up in these two short sentences: Salvation is all of the grace of God; damnation is all of the will of man."

Charles Spurgeon

If you enjoy Christian fiction, you might enjoy the series I completed last year called The Oberllyn Family Chronicles. It traces the stories of a single family through three centuries in America, past, preset times and future, with an eye on warning all those of us who love liberty and love the Lord what could happen to our freedoms if we don't guard them and pay attention to what is happening. The first book in the Series, <u>The Oberllyns Overland</u>, deals with the family at the time of the Civil war. *Here's the first couple chapters:*

"Well, mother, it's just about all I can stand," remarked Elijah Oberllyn as he stepped into the kitchen.

"What happened this time?" answered his wife Elizabeth. She was busy rolling out the dough for homemade noodles on the wooden kitchen table. Behind her on the woodstove was bubbling a rich broth to cook them in. From the oven came the wonderful smell of peach pie baking, and warm bread stood on the counter, covered in tea towels. Elizabeth was short woman, with her long black hair, just starting to show grey, done up in a bun at the back of her neck, wearing a solid brown apron over a calico brown dress, and she looked capable of taking on the entire army and feeding it at once. Bustling as she rolled out the dough, she reminded you of a wren on a branch, swaying and hopping from task to task, chirping merrily in between.

"That neighbor Jacks," began her husband. "He's let his cattle get into my wheat again. He says he'll mend the fence but this time he said it was my fault because if I hadn't planted wheat, his cows wouldn't have been tempted, and he is talking about suing me for tempting his cows!"

159

His wife looked at him and finally said, "You're serious? He is going to try suing you for tempting cows?" She started to laugh out loud but hushed herself when she saw how angry her husband was. "It appears to me the only person to benefit from that would be the lawyers."

"He wants my field to add to his farm. He won't mend the fences on purpose. He's expecting me to do his fence. He's doing the same thing to our son. He offered him a pittance for his orchard, and when Noah wouldn't sell, he started rumors about him being half crazed since the church kicked him out during the great Disappointment and not being right so some of our own neighbors are questioning us for having our own services and I simply am not sure what to do. It's bad enough he picks on us but really, taking off after my son is just about all I can stand." Elizabeth considered for a moment, then said quietly to her husband,

"It's not much of a witness to be fighting with the neighbors. Joe wants to go to California to hunt for gold, but Catherine is not about to drop everything for a wild goose chase. Noah seems content here. I haven't spoken to Mary or Emily about it. I suppose we could consider moving but I hate the idea."

"We've lived here peaceably with our neighbors for years. It's only since those Jacks moved into their uncle's farm we've had trouble. Our land is fertile enough, but when Jacks heard we'd tried to buy his uncle's farm once, he took a dislike to us. And now look." Her husband poured himself a cup of coffee and sat down, blowing on it to cool it, then looking at is wife with a pensive expression on his face.

"California is a right far piece to go," he started.

"Elijah! I was only giving you ideas from different members of the family, not saying I wanted to go." His wife turned with her hands on her hips, a distinctly displeased look on her face.

"It's a good idea and I might have to look into it. I don't want to be run out of town on a rail and that's just what that Jack's fellow is going to try and make happen. Besides, it's getting too crowded around here. It wasn't so bad before that train got put in. Now there are more people coming to buy land and settle in and it's just too crowded."

"Well, you need to pray about anything before you go off half-cocked," she said firmly. "Now go do your chores whilst I finish up supper."

Elijah went back to his barn and finished cleaning out stalls. His wife's jerseys would be up soon for milking. They'd cost him a pretty penny when he'd gotten them, but had proven to be just what Ma's dairy business needed. They gave rich milk, it made wonderful cheese and butter, and their farm was getting known for its good fruit and cheese. Until that neighbor had moved here, everything had been going along fine. Joe had a good thought, though. Out west, there was plenty of land and it wasn't crowded. They could worship as they pleased on Saturday and not be accused of being Judaizers or crazy or anything else. He had two more children at home and there'd be no land to give them as a farm of their own if he couldn't buy up some land. When his son Nathaniel got married, it was a good thing he was a doctor who hadn't time to farm. The farm was just too divided up as it

161

was, what with Emily and her brood, and Catherine and David over by the creek running the small fruits part of the family business. Miriam's man Joe being a lawyer had helped; they'd just needed land for a house and little garden for themselves, no real farming involved. Noah and Mary had taken over the fruit orchard and were making a good go of it, and he and Elizabeth still had enough for him to raise the best horses and oxen in the county and keep mom's dairy running, but they needed more land. It just couldn't be divided anymore and there was Thomas and Johanna yet to be grown and have a part. He supposed Thomas could inherit their home but where would Joanna go? And that Jacks trying to force them to sell land to him they didn't have to spare, he and his dirty tricks. Hard to imagine what he'd try next. Maybe Joe had a good idea. *I believe I'll just visit the land office and find out about land west of here. It surely wouldn't be bad to have a look.*

He came out of the barn and stretched. His son Thomas came dashing up; that child never went anywhere at a walk, always running. "Pa, you got a letter."

"Oh? Thank you, son. Let's have a look." He took the letter from him. It was an official looking document from the US government.

"Haven't seen one of these since well before you were born."

"Was that back when you and mama lived in New York?"

162

"Yes, pretty much when you were a baby, before grandpa died and we inherited the farm."

"Wonder what they want?"

"Whatever it is, your mom and I will deal with it. You're supposed to have seen to the goats."

"Done. You know the mom angora is going to give birth any day?" he grinned. "Can't wait to see them. I love the way the babies sprong around."

"Well, you keep a good eye on her."

Thomas hesitated. "Pa, I saw Mike Jacks over looking at mom's sheep. He had this funny look on his face?"

"Funny like how?"

"He said his dad doesn't like sheep, they ruin the field. I told him it wasn't his field so not to worry about it. He said something under his breath and walked off. I don't like him much, pa. I was hoping for a friend that would move in that I could do stuff with but I don't think he likes me much."

"Don't worry about him. There are other folks to be with that don't cause such aggravation. Just be civil and leave him be."

"Yes, pa. He made Johanna cry. Oh!" he covered his mouth.

"What?"

"I wasn't supposed to tell you."

"Stop right now. You don't keep secrets from me, ever. When was Johanna crying?"

"She went out to get the cows yesterday and Ellie Jacks was waiting and called her a cowgirl and teased her about her hair."
"What's wrong with her hair?"

"It's sort of red, I guess. And Johanna was crying when she helped with milking."

"I see. And you weren't supposed to tell me?"

"Johanna said we were having enough trouble with this family and God wouldn't want her complaining about it."

"I see. Well, you just let me handle this. Must be about time for supper, yes, there's mom ringing the dinner bell. Let's go wash up."

Dad and Thomas washed up at the pump and went inside, hanging their hats by the door.

"That smell sure chirks a fellow up, ma. Can't wait to have some of your chicken and noodles." Elizabeth smiled.

"Johanna, would you mind getting the field tea I made? I put it in the springhouse to get cold." Johanna nodded and went out the door, coming back with a pitcher covered in a towel.

" Mom," she frowned. "I don't think we ought to use the tea."

"What's the matter?"

"Somebody's been in the spring house."

"Really? How do you know?"
"The cheese's are all on the floor and the milk's spilt." Ma and Pa rushed outside to the spring house where they found rounds of cheese scattered all over, the five gallon milk cans flipped, polluting the spring run over. They looked around at the damage. Ma shook her head.

"I hate to think we'd have to put guards on our home, but this is outrageous."

"If we tell the sheriff," began Thomas.

"He'll say it could've been done by animals, that someone left the door open. There's no proof."

"Why don't we make a list of what's going on at least and ask him to watch out with us?" asked Ma.

"We can do that. Are the cheeses ruined?"

"The shelves are broken down, but the cheese ought to be fine. I may have to rewrap some.."

"Let's see what we can do. Thomas - call Mick and Mike." Mike and Mick were the family mastiffs who spent most the time in the back field with the cattle. The dogs came to Thomas's call. "We'd best keep the dogs close to the yard or at least one of them here."

"Then who's going to protect the cattle from coyotes?" asked Thomas.

"It's not the four legged ones I am worried about just now."

Thomas and dad reset the shelves, and they helped mom wipe off the wax coated cheeses and set them back. While they did that, mom set the milk cans up and opened the overflow wide so the water could drain out and run clear. Finally they stood up and went out. Dad shut the door to the spring house and set Mike by the door, telling him to stay. He took Mick to the barn and set him there and they went inside to eat.

The meal was a quiet one. Ma and Pa were tight-lipped and Thomas and Johanna were quiet as they passed food around.

"I don't care what they say. Johanna, you have got the prettiest hair in the world. It shines in the sun like gold and when you wear your green Sabbath dress I have the prettiest sister in the county."

Johanna looked surprised and her eyes welled up. "Thank you," she whispered.

"I agree with your brother. I am not quite sure why he said it but thank you for noticing," said Pa. Mom and Johanna just looked confused. Suddenly, there was a loud meow from out back.

"What on earth!" said Ma, getting up. She went out back where a strange collie dog had her pet cat up a tree. She took a switch and chased it off. The dog ran to the end of the driveway where Mike Jacks was watching.

"Lady, you'd better not hurt my dog," he yelled at her.
"Then keep him on your own land," she replied.
"Well, this is going to be our land when my dad gets done with you," he yelled back. "You'd better not let those sheep overgraze it." Mom picked up a bigger switch and headed down the drive purposefully in his direction and he ran off. A passing wagon stopped.

"You all right, Mrs. Oberllyn?" said the farmer driving.

"I don't know, Zeb. We got neighbor problems. My spring house was attacked, they insult us and we just never did them any harm."

"I heard about some of that. Mr. Jacks was in the general store last week boasting he'd have your land soon. I don't know what he was talking about but I was coming to tell your husband if he was going to sell out, to call on me. I could use good fields like yours."

"I thank you, and I'll tell Elijah, but we have no interest in leaving our farm. It's been in the family for over a hundred years."

"Thought he might be blowing smoke. But still, keep me and my sons in mind. I'd rather buy from you than Jacks. Oh, and best be careful. There's some weird rumors going around." Elijah was on the porch and waved to his neighbor.
"Rumors?"

"I'm sure they ain't true. You say howdy to Elijah for me."
"Thank you, Zeb. By the way, did he happen to say why he wanted my land?"
"He said it was the best land in the district and I have to agree with him. Your orchards make the best fruit, your cheese is wonderful and you've always been real supportive of our community. Shame to have you leave."

"Aren't planning on leaving.."

"I hope not. Well, I best be getting home. You remember my offer."

Mom went to the back where Thomas had climbed the tree and gotten her Maine coon cat down. He jumped into her arms. "There, there, dear. I'm sorry he flustered you so. Shh, now. Shhh."

"Mom, why do they hate us?"

"I have no idea." They went inside. "We've never had this much trouble."

"Mom, did you know Jacks have got slaves?"

"What?"

"They have three of them. I saw them out working his field. And Mr. Jacks carries a whip."

"I see. Well, the good Lord never wanted slavery. We earn our needs by the works of our hands, not the sweat of others. Let's try to finish supper. It's most likely all cold by now."

Dear Lord,
Give me a few friends
who will love me for what I am,
and keep ever burning
before my vagrant steps
the kindly light of hope...
And though I come not within sight
of the castle of my dreams,
teach me to be thankful for life,
and for time's olden memories
that are good and sweet.
And may the evening's twilight
find me gentle still.

Old Celtic blessing....

Made in the USA
Middletown, DE
14 December 2019